Love You More

LOVE YOU MORE

MY FIGHT FOR JUSTICE
FOR MY DAUGHTER

JANET PELASARA

REGAN

An Imprint of HarperCollinsPublishers

All insert photographs courtesy of the author, except "Those Eyes," page 6, courtesy of Ed Solomon.

HarperCollins books may be purchased for educational, business, or sales promotional use. For information please write: Special Markets Department, HarperCollins Publishers, 10 East 53rd Street, New York, NY 10022.

For editorial inquiries, please contact Regan, 10100 Santa Monica Blvd., 10th floor, Los Angeles, CA 90067.

FIRST EDITION

Designed by Publications Development Company of Texas.

Library of Congress Cataloging-in-Publication Data has been applied for.

ISBN 10: 0-06-114595-5

ISBN 13: 978-0-06-114595-7

06 07 08 09 10   PDC/RRD   10 9 8 7 6 5 4 3 2 1

This book is dedicated to my mother.
She gave me courage and confidence, and she showed me what
real strength is. Real strength is enduring life's most painful
and never-ending heartache—that of losing the most precious
gift God could ever give, one's child.

CONTENTS

Love You More

1.

LEAVING HOME

In the summer of 2005 my daughter, Taylor Behl, seventeen years old and achingly beautiful, was getting ready to leave for college. She was only going as far as Richmond, Virginia, less than two hours from our home in Vienna, but I felt as if I was losing her forever.

Taylor, on the other hand, was bursting with excitement, and I managed to be excited for her. Still, deep down, I couldn't believe this was really happening. A week before she was scheduled to leave, I spent an entire day crying in my garden. It was the kind of crying where you can't catch your breath, the kind that just won't stop.

Parents go through this every year, I told myself. *Kids grow up. They go to college. You should be happy. It's a good thing.* But I couldn't shake the sad feelings. I knew they were compounded by the fact that I was a single mother, and that Taylor was my only child, but

I realized that this didn't make me unique. *All* parents went through it. We all wondered whether we'd done a good job of preparing our children for the road ahead. We all hoped for the best. We all worried.

In my own case, however, the anxiety seemed a little excessive. I'd always been a calm, levelheaded person, and this wasn't like me. I found myself contending with frequent optical migraines, along with the occasional panic attack, and every day seemed to bring fresh waves of anxiety.

I asked myself, *Is this some kind of mother's premonition? My sixth sense?*

One afternoon Taylor came home with a girl she knew from the local Starbucks, where they both worked, and suggested that I have her move in with me. "That way you won't be lonely when I'm gone," she said. She also made a habit of reminding all our adult friends that they had to look in on me from time to time. "I don't want to have to worry about Mom being lonely," she told them. And when I took her to see her pediatrician for one final check-up before school, she had this say: "I'm really excited about going off to college, but I don't like the thought of Mom home, alone."

"Honey, don't worry about me," I told her, laughing it off. "I'll be fine."

"But I *do* worry about you," she said. "I can't help myself."

I could feel the blood rushing to the back of my throat. "I love you," I said.

"Love you more," she replied.

On August 20 Taylor and I loaded both of our cars for the short drive to Virginia Commonwealth University, in the heart of

Richmond. We were going to spend the night in a hotel, get her settled into her dorm early the following morning, and I would then make the drive home without her, and *without crying*. We made good time, checked into our hotel, and parked our cars in the underground lot.

At dinner, I found myself staring at her across the table.

"What?" she said, smiling her bright smile.

"Nothing," I said.

I couldn't believe it: My little girl, almost all grown up. Where had the time gone? I had been Taylor's mother for seventeen years, and I would continue to be Taylor's mother, but my role was being sharply redefined. Who was I going to be without Taylor? I felt suddenly diminished, a lesser version of my old self, and I realized that I already missed her. I couldn't let it show, however; I smiled till my jaw ached.

After dinner, we decided to wander around the university to try to sneak a look inside her dorm. I had never been to the campus, so everything was new to me, and I liked what I saw. I began to feel more optimistic. This really *was* a good thing. Everything felt right. The night was clear, and not too warm, and the streets were filled with young, hopeful, wholesome-looking kids. Maybe some of them would become her new friends.

When we arrived at Taylor's dorm, one of the resident assistants (RA) was kind enough to show us to her room. It was small, designed for two people, and there was a tiny bathroom that separated it from a second, similar room. Taylor would be sharing the first room with a girl named Emma Ellsworth, whom she'd already met online. Emma happened to be an old friend of one of Taylor's closest friends, Glynnis Keogh, and I thought that was a good sign. She would be starting college with a solid connection to her life back home, and it would make for an easier transition.

"Tomorrow's going to be a madhouse," the RA told us. "If you want, you can move in tonight."

"That's a great idea!" Taylor said.

We returned to the hotel, got into our cars, and drove back to the dorm. It was a big, sweaty job. Taylor's room was on the third floor, and there was no elevator. Plus, she had brought tons of books, mostly classics, which was appropriate, I guess—she was there to study—but which were certainly tough on our backs.

We made her bed with her new sheets and her new comforter. Put her new towels in the bathroom. Hung up all of her new clothes. Set all her toiletries where they belonged. Even got her printer up and running.

When we were done unpacking, we went back to the hotel and collapsed, and the next day we got up, had breakfast, and returned to the dorm to meet some of the other students. Emma had already come and gone, but the two girls in the adjoining room were busy unpacking, and we introduced ourselves. I had made brownies for Taylor, and she shared them with the girls and their families. They seemed like very nice people. The girls were best friends from Woodbridge, Virginia, and their parents knew each other. We exchanged numbers and e-mail addresses and promised to get in touch.

At that point, there wasn't much left for me to do, and I got the impression that Taylor was eager to start her new life, so we wandered back to her room.

"Are you going to be okay?" I asked her.

"I'm going to be fine, Mom."

She looked a little sad, but I knew she was going to be all right, and I also knew it was time to go. I hugged her and kissed her and promised myself I wouldn't cry. I didn't have any tears left anyway—I had spent all of them in my garden—but I must have looked as if I was on the *verge* of tears.

"Oh Mom," Taylor said, "I am so sorry. Are you okay?"

"I'm fine," I said, and I gave her a big smile. "I want you to have as much fun as you can, but make sure you get good grades."

"I will," she said.

"Which part? The 'fun' part or the 'grades' part?" I asked.

"Both." She smiled.

She looked confident and happy and excited about the future, ready to start her new life as a college co-ed. I took her face in both my hands and stared at her. I think I was looking for a sign that she might not be ready, any little thing, so that I could take her back home with me. But she was ready, so I gave her a big kiss and turned and walked away.

I didn't even cry. I got in my car and drove to Roanoke, to look at a duplex that I'd been thinking of buying as an investment property. I didn't have any money to speak of, but I was hoping to use the equity in my townhouse for something with income potential, and I had a friend in Roanoke who said he'd be willing to manage the place if the sale went through. I met with the realtor, took a quick tour of the duplex, and drove home.

Three days later, Taylor called to tell me that she had strep throat and that she'd been put on antibiotics. She also told me that she had met a boy through one of her suite mates. His name was Jake Cunningham, and he was a freshman, too, and Taylor said she liked him because he was sweet and didn't drink or do drugs. Two days later, she called again to say that Jake had brought her flowers because she was still feeling sick.

"Isn't that the sweetest thing you ever heard?" she asked me.

"Yes," I said.

"He's really nice, Mom. A little clingy, maybe, but really nice."

Taylor came home that first weekend and filled me in on The Life of a Co-Ed So Far. Apparently, everything about it was terrific. Her teachers, the dorm, campus life, even her boyfriend, Jake, who played guitar and enjoyed sending her little love notes. She also liked her roommate, Emma, though she noted that their tastes were very different. Taylor had posters of Frank Sinatra and Johnny Depp over her bed, and she liked a range of music, from the Rolling Stones to Edith Piaf, while Emma was strictly into rock and rap.

"Now," Taylor said, pausing to take a breath, "will you please do my laundry?"

She went off to take a nap, still feeling sluggish from the antibiotics, and I went off to do her laundry.

When she got up, we went to dinner at the Sweetwater Tavern, a restaurant in Fairfax. Taylor liked one of the waiters—a very cute guy she'd actually gone out with once. After dinner, we went home and she went to bed early, and Sunday morning I did more laundry.

In the afternoon, Taylor's roommate came over so they could ride back to school together. This was the first time I had met Emma, and she hung out while I finished Taylor's laundry. Emma seemed a little shocked by the frankness with which Taylor and I communicated. Taylor was telling me about the partying and the drug use at VCU, for example, and about boys sleeping over in the dorm, and about a somewhat risqué version of spin the bottle that she'd said she'd only *heard* about, and I noticed the look of horror on Emma's face. "I can't believe you're sharing all these things with your mother!" she said.

"What?" Taylor replied. "She's my mom. I tell her everything." Then she added, in a very small voice, "*Almost* everything."

Before they left, we went to the grocery store and stocked up for the week. Taylor bought her usual junk food: Pepperidge Farm cookies (the double-dark chocolate and the Brussels), microwavable cakes, and lime-flavored Coke.

When Taylor and Emma took off, I went back to my life. I watched a little TV that night, crashed early, and on Monday morning I went back to work. I had a job as a contracts administrator with a computer services company, right there in Vienna. It was steady work, and it paid the bills, but it wasn't particularly inspiring.

Taylor and I didn't talk much that week. It was her first full week of school, and she was very busy, and I never wanted her to feel that she had to check in with me every day or even every other day. Many weeks later, however, I learned that she had made a remarkable impression on one of her professors. It was the professor's first day of teaching, and she was nervous, and the students were being horribly unresponsive, so Taylor began asking questions and managed to liven things up. When class was over, she took the time to tell the professor that she had really enjoyed the class, and that she was looking forward to the semester ahead.

When the professor wrote to tell me about it, many weeks later, she said that Taylor had gone out of her way to rescue her, and that she would never forget it. I wrote back to say that I expected no less from Taylor—and it was true. She had always been considerate, sometimes to a fault, even gravitating toward damaged, needy people. I had always loved that about her; I never thought that her big heart would be her undoing.

I saw Taylor again the following weekend, which was Labor Day. She came home on Sunday. She said she'd be at the house by 1:30 p.m., and I'd been invited to go swimming with one of my girlfriends, but I passed so that I'd be there when Taylor arrived. When she finally showed up, at 4:30 p.m., the first words out of her mouth were, "Mom, I have more laundry."

"Great!" I said. "Now I know what I'm going to be doing on Labor Day."

Taylor helped me separate the clothes and load the washer. She had a *lot* of clothes. I wouldn't describe her as a clothes horse, because she didn't like to shop, but whenever I managed to drag her to the mall she bought *everything*. As we sorted through her laundry, she told me about her week at school, and about a "cool" neighborhood place called the Village Café. She said she enjoyed hanging out there, especially after hours, but assured me that she never drank. She said she had met three guys at the café, Jesse, Ian, and a guy who worked there as a cook, and that she had gone skateboarding with them the previous Saturday. The sport was new to her, but she really liked it. "They told me I was pretty good," she said. "They said I'd 'caught some serious air.'" She had to explain this—it meant that the skateboard had been airborne, albeit briefly—and she stood there grinning, showing me some of the moves. Then she added a detail that disturbed me. "When I took a break from boarding," she said, "I passed out in Ian's car."

"What do you mean?"

"I think it was from the antibiotics. I'm still not over the strep."

"How long were you out?"

"Mom, it was nothing! Not even a minute. I think I just overexerted myself."

That evening, Taylor and her friend Glynnis and I went back to the Sweetwater Tavern for dinner. The cute waiter came over and asked Taylor if she would go to a concert with him on September 17. Taylor was seeing her new friend, Jake, but the relationship with the waiter had already defined itself as a simple friendship, so she happily accepted. I was happy, too. That meant I'd be doing laundry again on the seventeenth.

After dinner, the girls went to Glynnis's house and watched TV for a while, then went out to see *The Brothers Grimm*, starring Matt Damon and Heath Ledger. When Taylor got home, she went into her room to check her e-mail and found a Dear John letter from Jake. She came into my room shortly after midnight and woke me up to tell me about it. "I just got an e-mail from Jake," she said. "He broke up with me. I can't believe he broke up with me in an e-mail!"

"I am so sorry, Taylor," I said, hoping she would tell me more, hoping there was something I could do to comfort her, but she just went back to her room. I don't know why they broke up, and I still don't know, but Taylor had mentioned his clinginess from time to time, and I think she pulled away a little, and maybe Jake hadn't responded well. Or maybe it was something else entirely. All I know is that she was devastated, and that for hours afterward I could hear her in her room, at her computer.

Taylor spent a fair amount of time on her computer, and I knew she had a life online. She was into IMing (instant messaging), and she had an online journal, which she had posted on MySpace.com, a website. I didn't know exactly what it was, frankly, but I didn't want to pry. I assumed it was a personal diary. I didn't know she shared it with other people, or that complete strangers had access to it. But I wasn't worried about it. And even if I'd known exactly what it was, I still wouldn't have worried. I had complete confidence in Taylor, and complete trust. She was a smart girl. She wasn't going to do anything online that would get her into trouble.

Monday, she slept late. We were supposed to go out and get her a new bedspread, but we only had time for a trip to the grocery store. When we got back, she popped out to get gas, and when she returned she told me that it had cost her thirty-six dollars to fill the tank. I felt sorry for her and gave her forty bucks. She had money in an account of her own, of course, for her personal expenses, and she also had a food card to cover her meals at school, but I always enjoyed giving her a little extra, because she never asked and she was always grateful. She stuck the money in her back pocket, thanked me profusely— "Mom, you are the greatest!"—and kissed me good-bye.

"Drive carefully," I said. "I love you."

"Love you more," she said.

I stood at the door, as I always did, and watched her get into her car and drive away. She waved as she pulled out, beaming. That was the last time I saw her.

I turned around and went into the house, and for some reason I felt as if I'd been kicked in the stomach. I was literally doubled over in pain, so I made my way upstairs and crawled into bed. I didn't know what was going on. I had experienced occasional migraines during much of my adult life, along with fleeting, stress-related panic attacks, but this was the first time I had felt such intense, physical pain.

On her way back to Richmond, Taylor stopped briefly at her father's house to give him a poster of *The Shawshank Redemption*, one of his favorite movies.

At six o'clock that evening, my phone rang. It was Taylor, calling from school. "I'm here," she said.

"Great," I said. "Thanks for calling."

"Love you, Mom," she said, and she hung up.

I was still in bed, still in pain, but I got up and went downstairs and had a bowl of raisin bran. It didn't help. I went back upstairs, brushed my teeth, and once again crawled into bed.

In the morning, at work, I felt only marginally better, and I told a colleague about the previous evening. "The moment Taylor left, I felt, literally, as if I'd been kicked in the stomach," I said. "I guess I'm not too good at this empty nest thing."

That night, I went to dinner with a friend from New Mexico who was in town on business, and I got back to the house a little after midnight. At 3:30 in the morning, Wednesday, September 7, 2005, the phone rang. It was Officer Bill Butters from the VCU campus police. He didn't want to alarm me, he said, but Emma Ellsworth had called to report that she hadn't seen Taylor since Monday night. Emma had known Taylor for less than two weeks, but she didn't think Taylor was the type who would disappear without saying anything. What's more, Taylor's purse and her schoolbooks were untouched, and her bed had not been slept in.

Officer Butters said that Emma's call had come in at 1:30 that morning. She told the campus police that Taylor had returned to the dorm Monday, a little after 10:00 p.m., and that she, Emma, had been there with a boyfriend. Taylor decided to give them a little privacy, and she left, and Emma had not seen her since.

After her call, the campus police spent two hours checking various places, including the Village Café, Jake's dorm room, and the area where she normally parked her car. No one had seen her, and the campus police were unable to locate her car. "I just wanted to let you know that we're concerned, and that we're looking into it," Officer Butters told me. My immediate thought was that Taylor was dead, with her hands cut off. I have no idea why this horrific image came to me, but it was that specific: *Taylor is dead, and her hands have been cut off.*

2

PERSONAL HISTORY

I was born on October 7, 1960, in Arlington, Virginia, and I was such a tiny thing that everyone in my family called me Teenie. I had an older sister, Debbie, and two older brothers—Donald Jr., whom we called Bo, and Jimmy. We lived in Arlington until I was about six months old, then moved to Falls Church, where we stayed until I was four.

My father, Donald, was a policeman with Arlington County. He did a lot of work with juveniles and sex offenders, and growing up I used to read articles about him in the *Washington Post*. He worked his way up to detective, then sergeant, and ended his career as a lieutenant. At that point he decided that all along he had really wanted to be a motorcycle cop, so he went back and did that. He was a fun, life-of-the-party kind of guy, and he always seemed happy, and my mother, Nancy, was a happy, stay-at-home mom. She'd wake me up with coffee on a tray and ask me what I was wearing to school that morning, and whether it needed ironing, and if I wanted to start my day with eggs or cereal. Now tell me, wasn't I was the luckiest little girl in the world?

Before I turned five, the family moved to Broad Run Farms, in Loudoun County, just in time for the arrival of my little brother, Jeffrey. We had dinner at six o'clock every night, as a family, except on nights when Dad was working, and it was my favorite part of the day. I grew up dreaming of having a family just like my family, and right after I graduated from high school I married the boy whom I'd been dating since junior year. My goal—my *only* goal, really—was to begin having children right away, but countless visits to fertility specialists proved fruitless, and before long we were divorced and I had moved away to Fairfax. I had several jobs—dental assistant, personal trainer, aerobics instructor, receptionist—but none of them were particularly inspiring, mostly because I was so fixated on becoming a mother. I wanted to be just like my own mother, who had dinner on the table every night at six, scoured the local paper for good deals, and worried about the waxy yellow build-up on her kitchen floor.

In Fairfax, I rented a big house with a pool, and one day in the spring of 1985 the pool boy came over and never left. His name was Matt Behl. I thought he was one of the handsomest men I'd ever met, and he seemed very sophisticated to me. He was also very ambitious, and I realized that he was the kind of guy with whom I could build a family. There was only one catch: He had no desire to get married or have children.

Needless to say, it was a turbulent relationship. Matt could be very nice, but he could also be very mean, and we fought a great deal. The biggest issue for me was that he wanted his freedom—not to see other women, necessarily, but just to know that the door was open. By the fall of 1986, I had moved to an apartment in Springfield, and Matt and I were fighting more than ever, so I decided to give him his freedom.

Shortly after I'd sent him packing, I went out on a date with a guy I'd known for several years. He owned an appliance store in Springfield, and he was a perfect gentleman. When he brought me home at the end of our first date, Matt was waiting for me in my apartment, drunk and in tears. I told him to go to bed, and I apologized to my date and thanked him for a lovely evening.

In the morning, when Matt woke up, I made him coffee and prepared to send him home to his mother. The man had no intention of marrying me, or of having children, and I wasn't going to waste any more of my time. As I set his coffee down, I took a good long look at him. He was hung over and bleary eyed, but still incredibly handsome. "Marry me tomorrow or it's over forever," I said, knowing this would send him running. "You have eighteen minutes to decide." I don't know why I chose the number eighteen, but I guess it was as good a number as any—arbitrary, round, and solid.

"Couldn't we get married on the cruise?" he asked.

We had scheduled a cruise for November, before we'd broken up, and I hadn't realized that he was still planning on going. Not that it made any difference—I wanted an answer *now*. "No," I said. "You have seventeen and a half minutes to decide."

"How about at Christmas—that's only three months away?" he asked.

"Nope. Tomorrow."

He had a sip of coffee, looked me in the eye. "Okay," he said. "Yes."

"Excuse me?"

"I said *yes*. Let's get married."

Amazing. He still had seventeen minutes to go.

That was a Sunday. We spent the afternoon shopping for wedding bands, and I remember feeling very happy. The way I saw it, Matt had responded to my ultimatum because he loved me and didn't want to lose me. It had just taken a small push to make him aware of it. I also knew, without asking, and without discussing it with him, that there would be children in our future. *Lots* of children.

On Monday morning, we drove to nearby McLean and were married by a justice of the peace. The justice provided a witness for a nominal fee.

A few seconds after I said "I do," I almost passed out. I was kind of shocked that I'd actually gone through with it. I thought I loved Matt, but I wasn't really sure, and I wondered if what I really loved was the idea of being married and having children. In any event, we had both said yes, on cue, so there we were—married.

Matt and his business partner were just starting out back then, and the company's main order of business was managing community pools. But things quickly improved, and before long we went off to buy a townhouse in Springfield, about a mile and a half from Matt's mother's house. The night we moved in, we had a big fight. Matt said it was his house because he had paid for it, but my income had helped us qualify for the loan, so my name was on the

4.

MISSING

Taylor was thrilled about going off to VCU, and equally thrilled over her imminent graduation from high school. We decided to throw a party, and we planned it together. We spent weeks making the invitations, and Taylor insisted on putting upbeat, life-affirming messages on each of them. *Life is a celebration. This is a time for happiness. The future has never looked brighter.* That type of thing.

Grammie Dearest, a.k.a. Ivy Stewart, flew up from Pawley's Island two weeks before the party, to help me organize it. We were having it at the house, and I wanted the back yard to look perfect, which meant laying slate and installing new outdoor lights—which I did on my own. Grammie helped me with the shopping, which meant finding the exact tablecloths and paper plates to match. The morning of the party, which we held on the Saturday before graduation, our cousin Mike Davis showed up with a thousand dollars' worth of flowers. He was in the catering business, and he had worked a party the night before, so he got a great deal on the flowers—they were free.

The party was a huge hit. Forty or fifty people showed up. Half of them were kids from school, and the other half were family and friends, including her father, Matt. We had hired a couple of young kids to work outside as valets, because parking was limited, and I had asked a friend from work, Rob Johnson, to tend bar. We served shrimp, brisket, and pasta salad, and something called Poor Man's Meatballs, which you prepare in a Crock-Pot with ketchup and grape jelly. I know it sounds revolting, but it's actually pretty good—and Taylor had requested it. We also served a little wine, wine coolers, and beer to the kids who were over eighteen, but most of them were more interested in sodas.

The party lasted into the wee hours, but I actually went to bed around midnight. I'd like to say that I was simply being a perfect, considerate mom, giving my daughter and her friends their privacy, but the truth is that I was exhausted, partly because I was already anxious about Taylor's move to Richmond. In some ways—to me, anyway—the party felt like a good-bye party. It was a little overwhelming, to be honest, and it made me sad. Grammie stayed up and chaperoned, however, and by the time I got out of bed in the morning she had already cleaned up. There was no sign that we'd even had a party. Thank God for Grammie Dearest!

"Those were the nicest kids I ever met," she told me.

"Yes," I agreed. "Taylor has wonderful friends."

When Taylor got out of bed, she was beaming. She came over and hugged me, still smelling of sleep. "That was the greatest party ever, Mom! Thank you, thank you, thank you! You're the best." She even wrote me a very sweet thank-you note.

After breakfast, we sat down—Grammie, Taylor, and I—and she opened her presents. There were so many of them that I had to keep track of what she'd received from whom, so that she could write proper thank-you notes. Some people had given her envelopes with cash, and in her thank-you notes to those people she wrote exactly the same thing: "I promise I won't spend it on beer and pizza!" She liked pizza, but she never drank beer, so I knew that was at least half right.

The present she wanted from me I couldn't afford: it was a collection of Victor Hugo's work, *Les Misérables,* in French, and it was selling for a thousand dollars. Instead, I gave her five hundred dollars, and in my note to her I said, "This is for beer and pizza." I figured if she wanted the Victor Hugo collection badly enough, she was already halfway there. And if she didn't want it, five hundred dollars bought a lot of pizza.

The following week, we went to her graduation ceremony. Grammie and I sat in one section, and Matt and Carol sat elsewhere. At this point, things were a little strained between us, partly because Matt had decided, unilaterally, to cut the last two months of child support—ostensibly to help offset the cost of college. Taylor was about to turn eighteen, so I was effectively down to my last two payments. I was also upset with Matt because he had never offered to help defray the cost of Taylor's party, even though he was invited and showed up and enjoyed himself. Finally, he had promised Taylor a trip to Australia, then changed it to Hawaii, then decided that instead of a vacation he would give her a laptop computer, which she needed for college anyway. But the broken promise of an exotic vacation was another disappointment for Taylor.

Still, when all was said and done, these were relatively minor issues. I was more consumed by the notion of Life After Taylor. I knew she was only going to be an hour and a half from Vienna, but the thought of letting her go was emotionally crushing, and there were days when I felt that the world was coming to an end.

During the graduation ceremony, however, I decided not to think about any of that—not about Matt, not about Taylor's imminent departure—and I genuinely enjoyed myself. Taylor was glowing when she went up to receive her diploma, smiling her big smile, and I was the proudest mother in the world (well, *one* of them, anyway).

After the ceremony, Taylor and her friend Glynnis Keogh went to the all-night graduation party thrown by the community, and they made a karaoke video. She and Glynnis got up and sang "I Can't Get No Satisfaction," which still ranked as one of Taylor's all-time favorite songs.

The following week I told Taylor about her father's decision to cut off the last two months of child support. I was still pissed off at Matt, for that and for all those other reasons, and I had always been honest with Taylor about my feelings. Still, I wanted to do something positive with my anger, and I came up with a brilliant idea. Taylor had been talking to me about getting a tattoo, and it seemed to me that opportunity was knocking. "The last child-support payment comes in August," I said. "We should use it to pay for your tattoo."

I knew it was a little small-minded—*Revenge of the Angry Ex-Wife*—but I also knew that Taylor would be getting a tattoo before long, with or without my approval.

"Oh Mom!" she said, throwing her arms around me. "That is so great! You are awesome and Dad will hate it!"

We went to visit a dozen tattoo parlors together, but Taylor couldn't decide what she wanted. She figured that when she saw the perfect one it would jump out at her, but none of them ever seemed quite right, and she decided to be patient—to keep looking. She never found the right one.

Before summer ended, I financed a short, solo vacation for her to New York, per her wishes. She went to stay with Margaret Stockton, the daughter of Elizabeth Stockton, our old neighbor from McLean, and she fell madly in love with Manhattan. She found the city incredibly vibrant and wonderfully exciting, and she loved being surrounded by so much energy. She went to listen to a concert in Central Park because one of the bands from Jammin' Java was playing there, and she did a lot of sightseeing: Central Park, the Empire State Building, the South Street Seaport, the Statue of Liberty, Greenwich Village. She also went shopping, a must in New York City, and bought herself a pair of high-top tennis shoes decorated with dragonflies. Before she had even left the store, she called to tell me about them: "Mom! You'll love them! They are the bee's knees!"

Taylor also spent an entire night in line outside a Midtown bookstore, determined to be among the first people to get the latest copy of the Harry Potter series. (It wasn't even for her; it was a gift for Glynnis.) And when she came home, full of wonderful stories about the city, she was already planning ahead: "When I finish college, I am definitely moving to New York."

In early August, we took one final vacation, just the two of us. There was a huge "tip jar" in our house, where I always put my change, because I didn't like the way it weighed everything down, and we sat down at the kitchen table and stacked the coins into tidy rolls for the trip to the bank. It added up to more than four hundred dollars, and we used the money to visit Ocean City. We went to the beach, ate out a lot, and visited every tattoo parlor within twenty miles of Ocean City, looking for just the right tattoo. Alas, Taylor still couldn't find what she was looking for.

At about that time, Taylor added the following entry to her profile on MySpace.com: "I just graduated from high school and now I'm off to Richmond. . . . I'm looking forward to meeting people that are in Richmond because I only know a few people down there. But I love to meet new people in general so feel free to message me whenever to chat!"

She didn't get a chance to meet too many new people. Two weeks after she left for college, so full of hope, I woke to the ringing phone. I knew it was bad—the police never call in the middle of the night with good news—and that terrifying thought popped into my head. *Taylor is dead, and her hands have been cut off.*

I was later told that nothing had been done to Taylor's hands, but for some reason I couldn't get rid of the image. I wondered whether it was perhaps connected to my own feelings of powerlessness.

After I got off the phone with the police, I called Taylor's friend Mike Cino on his cell phone. It was 3:30 a.m., and it was clear I had woken him. I told him about my brief conversation with the VCU police, and asked him if he had any idea where Taylor might be. Cino told me that he hadn't spoken to Taylor in a long time, adding that he was actually in Vienna, not in Richmond, and that he was sorry he couldn't be more helpful.

I went downstairs and paced around the house, trying to make the center hold, and after a few minutes I decided that I needed to be in Richmond. I took a quick shower, jumped into my car, then stopped at the 7-Eleven for coffee. When I was still thirty minutes from Richmond, I called Matt. "I'm on my way to Richmond," I told him. "Taylor's missing." Matt's first thought was that she had run off, so I had to set him straight. "No, Matt. You don't understand. The police called to tell me she's *missing*."

I asked him to go into her bank account to see if she had withdrawn any money in the last forty-eight hours. He hung up, went online and checked, and called back in a few minutes. "Nothing," he said. "No recent activity."

I got to VCU at about six o'clock, made my way to the building that housed the campus police, and met with Officer Bill Butters. He didn't know anything yet—just what he'd already told me. I asked him about the local hospitals, which they hadn't checked yet, and I asked about her car.

"We haven't found the car yet," he said. "We're looking." He then asked me for a recent picture, went off to make a copy, and returned with the original a few minutes later. Officer Butters asked me what Taylor had been wearing when I last saw her, on Monday, Labor Day, and I told him that she left the house in jeans, a black T-shirt, and a black, hooded sweatshirt.

At that point, I was calm and unemotional; you might even say I was *removed*. I wanted to be able to process everything they shared with me, even if it made no sense. At one point, for example, they tried to tell me that Taylor might have run off with friends, which they said was not unusual. "A student is reported missing and shows up unharmed a few days later," I was told.

"Not Taylor," I said. "She's not that type of kid."

When I left the campus police, I walked the half block to the Village Café, where Taylor had been seen two nights earlier, having dinner with her friend Jake Cunningham. It was only eight o'clock in the morning, but the place was already open, and someone introduced me to the owner. I told him that Taylor was missing and I showed him her picture. I also told him that Taylor had written me to tell me how much she liked the café, and to say that she often hung out there after hours. The owner became quite defensive. He assured me that the only people allowed in the café after hours were the employees. He did tell me, however, that he had a video camera trained on the bar and restaurant area, which was timed to begin recording after hours. "When the manager comes in, I'll have him look at the tape," he said. "And I'll let you know if she's on it."

I went back to the campus police station, borrowed the local phone book, and started dialing the emergency rooms at the city's various hospitals. There was no sign of Taylor in any of them. Then Officer Butters told me he was going to talk to Jake Cunningham, with whom he'd already spoken once, albeit briefly, and wondered if I wanted to go. I did. We drove over to Jake's dorm and went to his room. It was the first time I had met him. He was a nice-looking young man, eighteen years old, and he repeated what he had already told the officers: Taylor had been with him at one of the campus classrooms, helping him finish an art project—Taylor was *always* helping people—and when they were done they had gone for dinner at the Village Café. After dinner, they went their separate ways, and he hadn't heard from her since. We thanked Jake for his time and returned to the precinct.

We got back in the middle of a shift change, just as a burly, black officer made his way inside. He walked softly, purposefully, and with confidence, and I went up to him and asked in a child-like voice, "Are you going to find my daughter?" He turned and looked at me, and I guess he could see that I was desperate for re-assurance. "Yes, ma'am," he said gently. "We will." That was exactly what I needed to hear.

By this time it was after ten in the morning, so I called my office back in Vienna and said I wasn't coming in. I told them that Taylor was missing, and that I was in Richmond. They asked if there was anything they could do, and I told them no, not at the moment, and I thanked them for being so understanding. I then went outside and got in my car, charged my cell phone, smoked several cigarettes, and tried to think positive thoughts. *Taylor is all right. Everything is going to be fine. My little girl will be home soon.*

When I was done smoking, I went back to the Village Café and got a scrambled egg sandwich, a glass of orange juice, and coffee—lots of coffee. I was operating on less than three hours of sleep.

After breakfast I returned to the precinct, hoping for news, but there was nothing to report. A short time later, Courtney Campbell and Rob Johnson arrived from my office in Vienna to see what they could do to help. We not only worked for the same company, but Rob had tended bar for me at Taylor's graduation party. It was nice to see a pair of familiar faces.

Within an hour Rob, Courtney, and I were being chauffeured around Richmond by a female officer, looking for Taylor's car. The campus police said they had put out an All Points Bulletin on the car, but it hadn't surfaced, and they wanted us to help them look for it on the neighboring streets. We didn't find it. We also stopped by Taylor's room at the Gladding Residence Center, across West Main Street from Monroe Park, on the off chance that I might stumble across a helpful clue, but there was nothing—the room appeared disturbingly normal. I had been in that very room only two weeks earlier, helping Taylor get organized. I had set up her printer. I had made her bed. I had put her things away in those drawers. *Where was my daughter?*

I noticed that Taylor hadn't taken her purse, her wallet, any clothes, or even her medications—which included her antibiotics, her birth control pills, and her antidepressants. "Taylor is not the type of girl who can stay in the same clothes for several days in a row," I said, turning to face Rob and the female officer. "She likes regular showers and frequent changes of clothes. And she didn't take any of her things. I think it should be pretty obvious that we're not dealing with a runaway."

At this point, the female officer asked if we'd accompany her to Ben Fawley's house, to see if he might talk to us. The campus police had already been there, too, having been informed that he and Taylor were acquainted, but Fawley had told them that he didn't know anything, and that he hadn't seen her recently. The police felt that he might be more forthcoming if I was with them, and I was only too happy to help. I had never met Ben Fawley, but I had heard about him from Taylor, of course, who showed me the pictures he had taken, and I'd had a brief exchange with him some months earlier, on Taylor's computer.

We went to his house and rang the bell. A moment later, Fawley came to the door. He was thin, with blond hair and a matching goatee, and there was something creepy and unclean about him. I disliked him instantly. He said that the police had already been there several times, and repeated what he'd already told them: "I have no idea where she is." Then he turned to me and said in a raised voice, "You don't know anything about your daughter. She's not the good little girl you think she is." I felt suddenly, violently ill, and I had to walk away. What was he suggesting? Why would he say such a thing about Taylor? I knew my daughter. My daughter was a good, decent, caring girl. What kind of person would say a horrible thing like that, especially at such a difficult time?

We left and got back in the car, and I was of course very upset, but I kept my emotions under control. We continued to drive around, checking parking lots, looking for Taylor's car, and at this point I began to feel that the campus police weren't as invested as they should be. Maybe the aimless driving around had something to do with it—*Where was this going?*—and maybe it was connected to Fawley's creepy comments. I'm not entirely sure, to be honest, but when we got back to the campus police station I immediately asked the officers whether they'd been in touch with the local and state police. I was assured that everyone was in the loop, but something didn't ring true, and I wanted confirmation. So I called the Richmond Police and spoke to Officer Trish Hamilton, and she told me she could find nothing in the system regarding Taylor. I was exasperated, and I was beginning to get angry. When I got off the phone, I confronted the campus police, and they assured me that there was an APB out on Taylor, and on her car, and that it was being broadcast on the radio every hour on the hour. I still wasn't satisfied, but I didn't know where to turn. It occurred to me that I hadn't heard from Matt, so I went outside and lit a cigarette and called him. "It's me," I said.

"Is she still missing?" he asked.

"Yes," I said. "She is still fucking missing! She hasn't run away and she's not off on a jolly! She's *missing*." I didn't wait for his response. I just hung up.

Courtney left for home—she had a toddler waiting for her—and Rob and I went back to the Village Café for dinner. I had no appetite, however, and barely picked at my food. While I was there, I asked, again, if anyone had seen or heard anything about Taylor, but no one had a clue. I also asked about the skateboarders—the three boys Taylor had mentioned during her visit home—but they weren't around.

Rob and I sat in the same booth Taylor had shared two nights earlier with her friend Jake. I pushed my uneaten dinner aside and reached for my cell phone and called T-Mobile. I told the operator who I was, and said I was trying to determine the last calls Taylor had placed and/or received. Since Taylor's phone was in my name I had no trouble getting their help. Her last incoming call had been at 9:45, from Tony, a friend on campus. There were no calls to or from Ben Fawley, or Jake, or to or from anyone else who might know anything.

After dinner, I finally got the nerve to call my mother, who was now living in South Carolina, near my brother. I had avoided doing so because I wasn't ready to admit that this was really happening. If I didn't acknowledge it, especially with those closest to me, I could go on telling myself that I was simply trapped in a horrible nightmare.

"Hello?" my mother said, picking up the phone.

"Mom, what are you doing?"

She started talking about her day, but I cut her off. "Mom," I said, blurting it out. "Taylor's missing."

"Oh dear God!" she said, gasping.

Hearing those three little words, hearing that emotion in her voice—that's what finally did it for me. *I'm never going to see Taylor again,* I thought. *I am never going to see my little girl again.* It was as if Taylor had just died for the second time. She had died on that first phone call, and she had died again on this one.

I tried to be strong. I told my mother that the police were doing all they could, even though I felt that they weren't doing anywhere near enough, and that I would call her the moment I heard anything. She asked if she should come to Richmond, and I told her no—that I'd manage. "But please let everyone know what's going on," I said.

When I hung up, I realized that I had just asked my mother to share the terrible information with the entire family, and it struck me that there had been nothing on the news about Taylor. It further occurred to me that I needed to share the information with the *entire world*. If everyone knew, everyone would help me find her.

Rob and I returned to the police station and I told the officers about my conversation with T-Mobile. I gave them the last few numbers that showed up on Taylor's phone log. They thanked me and said they would look into it, and one of the officers went off and got to work on the phone numbers right away. I then borrowed one of the computers at the precinct, logged onto my account, and began sending e-mails to everyone I knew. I told them Taylor was missing, and that she hadn't been seen since Monday night at 10:20 p.m. "If anyone hears from her, please let me know," I wrote. While I was still online, one of my friends responded, asking if this was some sort of sick joke. "No," I replied, "I wish it was."

When it got dark we went to look for the skateboarders, who were always getting chased away by the police and seldom came out before nightfall. Once again, we were driven around by the female officer. We found a few skateboarders at the first place we stopped, and we showed them Taylor's picture, but none of them recognized her. We tried a few more hangouts with similar results.

By this time, it was after 10:00 p.m. and I was operating on nervous energy. Rob and I went to the 7-Eleven, picked up two toothbrushes, and set off in search of a hotel. The hotels were mostly booked—there was a big NASCAR rally in Richmond that weekend—but we found one room with two beds. When we got upstairs, I barely had enough energy to brush my teeth.

"You all right?" Rob asked me, looking concerned.

"I don't know," I said, and I crawled into bed and collapsed. I was so exhausted I actually slept through the night.

The next morning, another colleague, Michael Smith, showed up at the hotel. He had arrived in Richmond late the previous night, with his dog, and they had slept in his car. Now here he was in our room, with his laptop computer, ready to get to work. He began by designing a flyer—it included a picture of Taylor and a second, smaller picture of her car—and by putting together a list of contact numbers, emergency and otherwise. He was appalled that I didn't have my laptop, so he went out and bought another one, as well as a printer, along with some good quality paper for the flyers. Then he returned to the hotel lobby and reconnected with Rob, and the two of them got to work.

I then called my cousin, Ann Martin, and her husband, Mike Davis, in Vienna, asked if they would come down and help me look for Taylor, and if they could stop by my house en route and bring me some clean clothes. They were there within two hours. As soon as they arrived, Ann began to look for a hotel that was willing to accommodate all of us, along with Michael's dog. The Marriot had one room left, and the sympathetic management gave it to us at a reduced rate.

This was Thursday, September 8. As soon as we checked into our hotel room, I called the *Times-Dispatch*. I was put through to Jim Nolan, one of their reporters, and he told me he would be more than happy to write a story about Taylor. He gave me his e-mail address, and I sat down at my computer and tried to reconstruct the previous thirty-six hours.

Meanwhile, Michael Smith and Rob had finished designing the flyer. Mike Davis, Rob, and Ben—a friend of Rob's—then took the flyer to Alpha Graphics, a local print shop, and printed up several hundred copies. The owner gave them a generous discount. Rob and Ben left the store with the first batch and raced around campus, putting them on doors and windows and trees. Strangely enough, someone was taking them down almost as quickly as they got them up. Rob and Ben said it was probably the university, worrying about the bad publicity, or about the effect the news would have on its students.

I then called two local TV stations to tell them who I was and what was going on, and that evening both of them showed up at the Marriot to speak with me. Mike Davis and I went downstairs to meet the reporters. This was the first time in my life I had ever been in front of a camera, and I was anxious, but I felt I *had* to do this. The moment I started talking I forgot that the cameras were even there, and it felt like the most natural thing in the world. I was there to bring my daughter home, and that's all that mattered. I did two interviews, back to back. I told the reporters the little we knew about Taylor's disappearance, and I asked for the public's help. I described Taylor—five feet six inches tall, brown hair, big smile—and described what she'd been wearing the last time I'd seen her: blue jeans and a black, hooded sweatshirt.

I was trying very hard to be strong, and I got through both interviews without crying. The reporters told me I'd done a great job, and then they got into their news vans and left. I turned to Mike and asked him if he thought the publicity would help. "Definitely," he said. "You were great."

After the interviews, I tried to keep busy. I didn't want to obsess about what was happening, or what might have already happened—I didn't want to think about the unthinkable. It occurred to me that I hadn't heard a word from the VCU administration, and I called the campus police to ask them about this. "I'm completely in the dark," I told them. "I have no idea what they're thinking or what they're doing, if anything. All I know is that someone has been ripping down our flyers, and I can only assume it must be them."

I was told that an administrator would get back to me, but no one did. Then my cousin, Ann, made a call to someone she knew who knew the school president, and not long after I received a call from Dr. Ruben Rodriguez, the vice-provost. He told me how sorry he was, and said I shouldn't worry—that the campus police were doing everything in their power to find Taylor. He then asked if there was "anything else" he could do. I was totally speechless. The one thing they had done, quite effectively, was to rip down our flyers. I was so upset that I handed the phone to Ann and said, "I cannot talk to this man."

Ann took the phone again—I walked away—and she managed to get results. They agreed to meet with us in the morning, to make copies of the flyers, and even to help us put them up. They assured Ann that this time the flyers would *stay* up.

I was still fuming when I went to bed. I didn't understand where Dr. Rodriguez got the nerve to ask me if there was anything else the school could do. They weren't doing a single thing. In fact, we seemed to be working at cross purposes.

I was so upset, and so exhausted, that I completely shut down, and once again I managed to sleep through the night.

On Friday, September 9, there was a brief article in the *Richmond Times-Dispatch*. It appeared without a byline:

A Virginia Commonwealth University freshman has been reported missing, university officials said yesterday.

VCU police said Taylor Marie Behl, 17, of Vienna in Fairfax County, was last seen leaving her dorm room around 10 p.m. Monday. Also missing is Behl's car, a white 1997 Ford Escort with Virginia tags JPC-2848.

Behl is 5 feet, 6 inches tall, weighs 135 pounds and has brown hair. She was last seen wearing blue jeans and a black, hooded sweatshirt.

Police said they do not suspect foul play. They ask anyone with information on Behl's whereabouts to contact them at (804) 828-1196.

I was disappointed. I wanted more.

Later that morning, friends and family continued to show up— my friends Kay Rosenthal, Tracy Nelson, and Denny Petrella; my cousins Karen and Wayne Martin, and their daughter, Beth, who lived in Vienna; another cousin, Ron Martin; and my friend Angela Armenakis, from Annandale. They walked around the campus, handing out flyers, and I helped out for a short while, then I went to my meeting with the administration. I took Ann and Mike with me for support, along with two cousins, Karen and Wayne.

Matt was already there. He had been contacted directly, and he was waiting in another room, but he had not been invited to our meeting. Those present included the head of the psychology department, the school's publicist, and of course Dr. Rodriguez. They assured me, *again,* that they were doing everything in their power to find Taylor, but their words reeked of cliché. I found myself getting more and more upset. Finally I stood up, shaking with contained rage, and said, "No decisions are to be made regarding Taylor unless I make them. I am the parent with sole custody and I will make any and all decisions."

At that point, I walked into the receptionist's office and basically fell apart. I cried hysterically and punched the wall and collapsed into a chair. The receptionist stared, not knowing what to do, then hurried off and fetched a glass of water. She handed it to me without saying anything. I thanked her, drank every last drop, and tried to regain my composure. I turned to look at the head of the psychology department. "I think I'm falling apart," I said. "I need something to get me through this."

He and Angie took me to the student infirmary, where I was seen immediately. The female doctor gave me a prescription for Zoloft and Klonopin and had both of them filled then and there. She explained that one was an antidepressant, and that the other was an anti-anxiety medication. The antidepressant would take a while to kick in, she explained, but the Klonopin should begin to work almost immediately. I took both medications on the spot.

We then rejoined Ann and Mike and some of our other friends, most of whom were busy passing out flyers. I remember deciding that I needed a moment to calm down, so I had a seat on a bench and lit a cigarette. A moment later, a young woman approached, introduced herself as a television reporter, and asked if she could interview me on camera.

"Of course," I said.

I talked about Taylor, and about all the friends who had come to Richmond to help find her, and I said I was trying to remain optimistic. I also told her about the flyers, which she'd seen, and about my meeting with the administration. "I don't think they're doing enough," I said. "Very few students even know my daughter is missing. The school has its own website. Why isn't her picture on it?"

The reporter didn't have an answer for me—how could she, the question was rhetorical—but she scribbled away furiously, then thanked me for my time and hurried off to file her story. The moment she left, another young woman approached me. "Are you Taylor's mother?" she asked.

"Yes," I said.

She told me she worked part-time at the Village Café, and that she had waited on Jake and Taylor on Monday night, the night she went missing. She said Taylor's dinner order had been sitting on the counter for a minute or two, and that she was just about to pick it up when Taylor left her seat and got it herself. She found that a little odd, the young woman told me, and she'd gone off and complained about it to the cook. "I don't know why she couldn't wait to be served, like everyone else," she had told him. The cook responded by rubbing his hands together, with glee, and mouthing the words, *I love her.* "I thought that was pretty weird," the young woman said. "I just wanted you to know."

"Thank you," I said.

I agreed with her. It was weird and creepy. The idea that a middle-aged man would think about my young daughter in those terms was deeply troubling, especially since this was the same man with whom she'd recently gone skateboarding.

My friend Kay, whom I've known since I was five years old, was watching the interview, and when it was over she told me it was all she could do not to burst into tears. "You looked so forlorn, and so pitiful, and so vulnerable," she said. "I have known you my whole life, and I have never seen you look more fragile or more alone."

She urged me to eat something, and I had no appetite, but I forced myself to nibble on a peanut butter and jelly sandwich. Angela came over and sat with us, and suddenly I remembered that the cats were home, alone. I asked her if she could take care of them, and I gave her the keys to the house, and she drove back to Vienna right after lunch.

In the afternoon, as we continued passing out flyers, I ran into Matt and his sister, Dianne. They were also passing out flyers.

I did more interviews later in the day, and I made more calls, pleading with reporters to keep the story alive. I knew this was the only way we were going to bring Taylor home.

Friday night I collapsed again, escaping into sleep.

On Saturday, Wayne and Karen spent most of the day with Chief Willie Fuller, of the campus police, driving around, talking, and looking for clues. At the start of the day, Chief Fuller still thought that Taylor might have run off with friends, and that there was a good chance she'd be showing up imminently, but his conversations with Wayne and Karen finally convinced him, unequivocally, that Taylor was not the type of girl who would do such a thing. He couldn't have known this, of course, he didn't know Taylor.

There were, of course, things about Taylor that *I* didn't know, and some of them were brought to my attention by a group of Taylor's friends. They had stopped by the Marriot to offer their support, and they talked to me about aspects of her life with which I was not familiar. That was the day I learned that Taylor had a sex life, for example. I was told that Taylor had slept with four different men: A local musician, who lived in Vienna; the older brother of a friend from high school; Jake Cunningham, the fellow freshman she'd just met at VCU; and, finally, Ben Fawley. When I heard Fawley's name, I could feel my skin crawl. I had only just met him that week, and I had found him incredibly creepy. I had also been hurt and alarmed by what he'd said: "You don't know anything about your daughter. She's not the good little girl you think she is."

Much later, I spoke to Taylor's friend, Glynnis, about Taylor and Fawley, asking her whether it was true.

"Yes," she said.

"How do you know?"

"Taylor told me," she said. "I don't think she really liked him or anything, but she liked the fact that she was getting attention from an older man. She knew he was a little screwed up, but that's Taylor—she likes to fix broken people. I think he was more broken than she imagined, though, and after a while she didn't want to deal with him anymore."

I tried not to think about Ben Fawley, because the thought of him with Taylor was too disturbing. The idea that she had a sex life, however, and that she hadn't shared it with me, was a lot less troubling. I would have preferred to have learned of it directly from her, certainly not from her friends, but I had never expected Taylor to share every intimate detail of her life. My goal as a mother was to be there for her, and I'd like to think I succeeded. Taylor knew she could talk to me about anything.

In fact, the previous June I'd taken her to get birth-control pills. They were designed to help regulate her periods, but I also knew that sooner or later she was going to start having sex. I wanted her to be prepared for it, but I didn't want to be intrusive, so it was handled very casually, which is how I thought it should be handled. I was not one of those mothers who investigated every detail of her child's life. I trusted Taylor completely, because she had earned my trust, and we were very open with each other.

And it's not as if we hadn't talked about sex. Several of her friends were already sleeping with boys, and one of them had had an abortion, so Taylor was intimately aware of the pros and cons, even in the abstract. Still, she didn't have a real boyfriend, so she wasn't in a relationship that lent itself to sex, and she wasn't a drinker or a party girl, so I never imagined she would make a mistake that she'd come to regret.

Now, hearing about these liaisons, it struck me as odd that three of the four men were considerably older that Taylor. I remember how much this troubled me. I wondered what she was looking for. I wondered what was missing in her life.

Another friend informed me that Taylor had had a lesbian experience, and that she had even mentioned it in her online journal. The reference was somewhat coy, however, and the absence of detail made it hard to tell what had happened, if anything. Still, even if it had happened, I didn't think it was a big deal.

Chief Fuller also appeared at the Marriot that night, and he spoke to several of Taylor's friends. Those conversations only confirmed what he had already been told about my daughter, by Wayne and Karen, and by me: Taylor was a responsible girl. She would never run off without telling me. I had never suggested she was perfect because she was far from that, but she was a good and decent girl.

Just before Chief Fuller left that evening, he turned to me and said, "I'm going to ask for reinforcements."

The next few days were a complete blur. I remember my brother Jeffrey showing up, having driven all the way from Pawley's Island, South Carolina. I remember speaking to the campus police every day, several times a day. I remember calling the hospitals again, and I remember speaking to various reporters, some of whom had come in from out of town. Through it all, either Ann or Mike were always near at hand. They were there when I found myself spiraling downward, into the abyss, and they were there when I was on the edge of rage. I honestly couldn't have survived without them.

During one of my many interviews, a reporter told me that the press was amazed at my resolve. He said he didn't understand how I was managing to get through the days, day after day, without breaking down. "We're still waiting to see who's going to make you cry first," he said.

Oh I cried plenty, believe me, but not in front of the cameras.

My biggest concern was that I wasn't doing enough. I was pushing the media, and they had been reporting on the case, but with nothing new on the horizon they seemed to be losing interest. My cousin, Karen Martin, aware of my frustration, called her family lawyer, George O. Peterson. She explained the situation and he said he would be happy to do anything he could do to help me, pro bono. When we spoke on the phone, I liked him immediately. He had energy and confidence, and I needed that.

On September 14, Peterson had a brief conversation with a state representative, and followed it up with an e-mail:

As we discussed, I represent Janet Pelasara, the mother of Taylor Marie Behl. Taylor is a 17-year-old freshman at VCU. On September 5, 2005, at approximately 10:00 p.m., Taylor left her dorm room to give her roommate some privacy with her boyfriend. She left her dorm with her cell phone, her keys, and student I.D. She left behind her driver's license, her credit card, and her purse. Also missing is Taylor's 1997 Ford Escort with Virginia license plate # JPC-2848.

Taylor has not been heard from since September 5, 2005. There have been no calls from her cell phone. There is no activity on her credit card account. Taylor has not logged in to her personal website, http://www.myspace.com/doowop, since September 4, 2005.

Taylor was raised by her single mother, Janet Pelasara. She had an exceptionally close relationship with her mother. Taylor told her pediatrician before she left that she was very excited about going off to college, but that the one thing that worried her was leaving her mother alone. Taylor was very conscientious about keeping her mother informed of her whereabouts and even called her mother on September 5, 2005 to let her know that she had safely arrived back at campus.

Bill, Taylor is not a missing person. She had no means of running away—no credit card, no money, and no change of clothes.

Here are some links to some stories on Taylor. As you can see, she is an incredibly beautiful young lady. Anything you can do to help bring her back safely will forever be appreciated by both me and Janet.

He included the various links.

Also, at my urging, he sent a note to Ben Fawley:

Ben,

I am the attorney for Janet Pelasara. I would like to speak with you regarding Taylor Behl and see if you can give us any info on where she may be.

Please give me a call at 703-933-XXXX.

The following day, Fawley replied:

At this time I have given my statement to the police about everything I know about my friend Taylor Behl. I have been advised not to talk to anyone about this subject by the police. I am not saying that though I have nothing to hide and have given my statements freely to the police I am no longer speaking on the subject to protect both Taylor and myself. I will not speak to anyone about this topic unless I have an attorney who is representing me.

As I do not feel I have any reason to hire an attorney, as I have nothing to hide I will not be speaking to anyone more on this issue. All of Taylor's friends hope she is ok and we are all worried. However the police have my statement. I have nothing more I can add to this investigation.

Sincerely, Ben
(AKA: Skulz)

At that point, George Peterson decided to come to Richmond. We met in the hotel lobby, and I hugged him and I think that frightened him a little. Part of it was the situation, no doubt, and part of it was my evident neediness. But George was young and ready to get to work, and one of the first things he did was to help me deal with the media, which I desperately needed—this was all new to me. "You've got to be very careful about what you say to reporters, especially when you're naming names," he told me. "In these types of situations, there's always potential for defamation suits."

George then introduced me to Bubba Bates, a private investigator. He said Bubba would help me with anything I needed—from running errands to checking in with the police at regular intervals—and that I could always rely on him.

I then introduced George and Bubba to some of my friends—Kay, Tracy Nelson, Dawn Wolfrey, my brother Jeffrey, and everyone else. I was never alone, not even for a minute, and that's what gave me the strength to go on.

Jeffrey and I put together a list of all the people who needed to be kept apprised of any developments, or lack of them, and he took on the job of contacting them every night, either through e-mail or on the phone. To tell you the truth, it was something of a miracle that Jeffrey had made it to Richmond in the first place. He was a fireman, and he'd been injured on the job. His arm was in a sling, with six pins in it, and his back and legs were so battered that he was walking with a cane. But he didn't let the pain slow him down. He was there for me every step of the way, and he was usually at my side when I spoke to reporters. I was once questioned about Taylor's "worldliness," and about her preparedness for college life, especially in an urban environment, and Jeffrey was quick to answer for me. "Taylor is very smart and very worldly for a seventeen-year-old," he said, "But she is still a seventeen-year-old."

My sister, Debbie, out in Vacaville, California, wanted to fly out as well, but I asked her to stay home, and to take care of her own family. "I've got plenty of support at the moment," I assured her.

"If you need me, just call," she said. "I will get on the next plane."

Everyone around me was trying very hard to put their best face forward. They smiled and tried to look optimistic, but I could see the sadness beneath. Sometimes I could barely look at them without feeling as if I would burst into tears, but in an odd way that was comforting, too: Everyone was sharing my pain. If they could be strong for me, I would find the strength to go on.

The entire staff at the Marriot was also an incredible source of comfort and support. They treated me like royalty, and made me feel safe and secure, and it got to a point where I didn't want to leave the hotel. During one of my interviews, I had wanted to talk about the hotel staff to the press, to tell them how wonderful they'd all been, but the hotel manager advised me against it. "We want you to be safe," he said. "We don't want people to know where you're staying."

Still, I can tell you now that they went well beyond the call of duty during those very difficult weeks. They took care of my every need. Water, coffee, fresh towels, a local telephone directory. If I asked for a conference room, it was provided, along with food. In fact, food became a big issue. Everyone on the staff seemed to think that I wasn't eating enough, so they were constantly sending food to my room—on the house. Even the cleaning ladies were nice to me, and seemed to tiptoe around my pain and sorrow. One of them seemed to be down on her luck, so I gave her a bag of M&Ms and some fruit. She was so grateful that she almost burst into tears.

One night, the desk manager sent some chocolate ice cream to the room because he thought it might make me feel better—it did. And Laura, the bartender, kept me company when I stole off to the bar to have a smoke. She was incredibly attentive. If a story about Taylor appeared on the news, she would hush the entire room and crank up the volume and made sure everyone was paying attention.

They all reached out to me: the porters, the bellmen, the desk clerks, everyone. I have never been so hugged in my life. Every time I went to the hotel restaurant, where I ate every meal, it was another hug-fest. One of the waitresses gave me a pink bracelet with the word HOPE on it. "I know they're going to find Taylor," she said, and she gave me a hug, too. It got to a point where I simply didn't want to leave the hotel. I left from time to time, of course, to do an interview, or on one occasion, to go to the bank, but generally I stayed put. In fact, one night, George Peterson and my friend Kay were urging me to go out to dinner, saying they were tired of the same menu, and I gave it a try. But we were barely halfway down the block when I felt the beginning of a panic attack, and we quickly returned to my little Oasis of Caring.

In the morning, when I would go down for my morning cigarette, I was always greeted by the same bellman. He would set aside his personal copy of the *Richmond Times-Dispatch,* and he'd be waiting for me. "Did you read the paper yet?" he'd ask.

"No," I'd say.

"Well, you can have mine."

It was always nicely folded, and when he handed it to me he did so with a graceful little bow. One morning, as I got off the elevator, he was practically grinning. "There's a great picture in there," he said. I thought it would be a picture of Taylor, but it turned out to be an almost life-sized picture of my head. I was so shocked I screamed.

If I ever had doubts about people's innate goodness, and we all do from time to time, this experience dissipated them.

On September 15, Chief Fuller called to tell me that the Richmond police were going to be taking over the case. I was so relieved I wept with joy. There was a press conference that day, and I was invited to attend, and that's where I first met Rodney Monroe, the Richmond Chief of Police. I felt an instant connection to him, and I thanked him for taking over the case. I didn't have to spell anything out for him, either. He knew that my faith in the campus police had been dissipating with every passing day.

After the press conference, which was very brief, Chief Monroe issued an Amber Alert for Taylor, but he was forced to pull it because it didn't meet the required criteria. Apparently, an Amber Alert can only be issued if it is clear that an abduction has taken place, and that the person in question is in danger for his or her life. It was impossible for Chief Monroe to determine this, and he knew it, but he was serious about finding my daughter, and he had jump-started his investigation by going out on a limb for Taylor. I felt that we had made a giant leap forward. I truly believed that at any moment we were going to find Taylor.

That same afternoon, a Thursday, Chief Monroe sent several officers to Taylor's dorm and removed a number of items that he thought might help them with the investigation. These included her laptop computer.

Later the same day, the Federal Bureau of Investigation and the state police joined the search, and I was even more optimistic. They asked if they could remove Taylor's desktop computer from our home, in Vienna, and I called my mom, who had just arrived at my house, where she was going to be taking over the cat-sitting responsibilities from my friend, Angela. "The police are going to come by," I said. "Let them have anything they want." When the police arrived, they made a copy of the hard drive, and went off to scour it for clues.

At that point, in all honesty, I was only vaguely aware of Taylor's online journal. I had heard in passing about MySpace .com, and all of those other websites that were becoming increasingly popular, but I didn't really know how they worked. I imagined the authorities were combing through Taylor's computer for e-mails, and for anything else that might shed some light on the case, but this online world was still a complete mystery to me.

The following day, September 16, authorities went to Fawley's house and removed a number of items, including several computers. Jim Nolan, the local reporter, later spoke about this to NBC, noting that they had taken a lot more than a computer. "They came out with sex toys. They came up with whips and chains. A machete. A hatchet. A gun cartridge. A number of things that taken in isolation can make the imagination run wild."

The next day, the press went to town with the story. They noted that Fawley was obsessed with Goth imagery, that he fancied himself something of a photographer, and that he had a website called *Deviantart*. They said he seemed to be very interested in young women, and further noted that he had a "personal relationship" with Taylor. I wanted to defend my daughter, to explain that there was no relationship there, but Fawley had become the big story, and for the moment they were interested in him, not in anything the mother of the missing girl had to say. I suddenly remembered the conversation I'd had with Taylor weeks earlier. We were talking about how hard it was to really get to know another person, and how they often turned out far dif-

Taylor at eleven months

Taylor, at seventeen months, experiencing snow for the first time

Taylor's first trip to the beach at ten months old

I had this photo taken when Taylor was three.

Taylor with Kathy Nary—the woman who babysat her from the time she was nineteen months old until we moved to England when Taylor was five.

During our after-wedding dinner in Key West, Taylor wanted Trevor and I to smash the wedding cake in each other's face; instead she gently took the icing and smeared it on our faces. Here Trevor is giving her a little smear of her own.

Taylor, Trevor, and me at our wedding ceremony in 1992 on a trimaran at sunset.

Taylor at age six, along with Trevor and Spot in our kitchen in England

A family Christmas photo of Taylor, Trevor, and me in England in 1996

Taylor dancing with our friends Julie and Paul during their wedding reception. Taylor was a member of their bridal party.

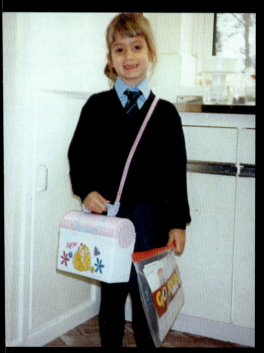

Taylor at five, heading off to school in Medmenham, England.

Taylor played T-ball in England when she was five.

Taylor at Windsor Castle with one of the Queen's guards

My favorite of her younger school photos, taken in England in her summer uniform at age five

Her fifth-grade school picture

This was taken before her etiquette dinner dance. Her escort, Brian, was a neighbor in Ashburn.

Ocean City, Maryland, 2000

Four generations—Taylor, me, my mother, and my grandmother. It was our second Christmas in America. Taylor looks so happy.

Christmases were usually spent in Florida with my mother. The pajamas we're wearing were a gift from her. We thought it was very funny to wear them to a neighbor's dinner party.

This photo was taken by professional photographer Ed Solomon when Taylor was fifteen. Entitled "Those Eyes," it won first prize in a state-wide professional photographers' contest.

Taylor and her friend Rob

Taylor and her best friend, Glynnis
Keogh, in front of Jammin' Java.

A profile shot of Taylor wearing her glasses and a ring I wore

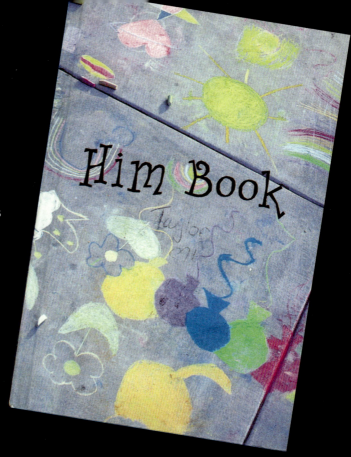

Pages from Taylor's "Him Book," which I gave her when she was around nine to write about boys she liked (or didn't like).

Taylor would often leave me little notes with her constant refrain of "Love you more."

The last Mother's Day card from Taylor and the last I will ever receive. This card shows her sense of humor and gratefulness and her love: "I Love You More!"

Jake Cunningham, Taylor's boyfriend at VCU.

A lovely note from Jake to Taylor.

Taylor,

Hii love.. Hope you slept well.

Love always,
Pancakes

Taylor in her new dorm room—the last photos I took of her.

February 02, 2006

Mrs. Janet Pelasara

Vienna, Virginia 22180

Dear Janet,

When the police asked for help in finding Taylor I told them yes I would do anything that might help. I had known Taylor casually and was alarmed by her disappearance. We spent hours going over photographs and looking at the sites in the pictures. We always hoped that we would find her alive. Finding Taylor has affected me in ways that I can't describe. I am so sincerely sorry for your loss. I wish that there was something I could do to ease your pain. The one thing that I can do is humbly decline your offer of the reward money for helping to find Taylor. Thank you for offering it to me. It just doesn't feel right to take money from you at a time like this. You are a woman of courage and determination. Taylor was blessed to have you.

Sincerely,

Erin Crabill

Erin Crabill

County/City of Richmond
Commonwealth/State of VA
The foregoing instrument was subscribed and sworn before me this 9 day of FEB 2006 by ERIN CRABILL

(Name of person seeking acknowledgment)

Notary Public

My commission 3/31/2008

I sent a reward check to Erin, and in this letter she kindly turns the money down. However, after much pressure from me, she eventually accepted the reward.

Dear Mr. Behl and Mrs. Pelasara,

11/14/05

I write this letter with my deepest sympathy.....

My name is Mary-Margaret Ruppel, and I was Taylor's VCU 101 teacher here at VCU. I felt compelled to write to you ever since Taylor was discovered missing to let you know what a sweet and caring daughter you had. Taylor made an immediate impression on me during the first day of our class. I was extremely nervous (for this was my first experience teaching) and I think that Taylor could sense my nervousness..... She was the first student to participate in our group discussion and to volunteer information about herself. Taylor made the class feel comfortable sharing a little bit about themselves. By setting out a comfortable environment.... and allowing everyone to relax with her reassuring smile and sweet laugh. Taylor even stayed after class once all of the other students had left to tell me she was looking forward to my course ....

May it comfort you

to know that others are

thinking of you

and remembering you

in their prayers.

and also not to be so nervous! Your daughter comforted me on that first day of class, and I'll never forget it. I'll remember her just as I did that September morning. You are all in my prayers. I am so sorry for your loss!

Sincerely,

Mary-Margaret & Ruppel

A note from Taylor's teacher remarking on how Taylor went out of her way to make her feel at ease on her first day of teaching.

Taylor took this picture of Ben Fawley in April 2005.

Crime scene photos

In Loving Memory of
Taylor Marie Behl

This is the funeral program. A thousand were printed and I have ten left. There was an amazing turnout for her service.

ferent than one imagined, and she'd said, "I know what you mean. I met a guy I thought was kind of interesting, but he turned out to be a real weirdo."

At that moment I knew that she'd been referring to Ben Fawley.

The next day George, the lawyer, logged onto Fawley's website and urged me to have a look. The name itself—*Deviantart*—scared me, but I braced myself and took a seat next to George. The photographs of Taylor were harmless, and I'd already seen them, anyway—on that CD she shared with me when she got home. But the rest of it—the imagery, the skulls, the ranting—gave me the creeps, and I refused to look further.

Then George showed me a picture that Fawley had taken of his own daughter, a girl of twelve. She was in a school uniform, and posed like a young Britney Spears. It was very sexual and very disturbing.

In the afternoon, while we were busy setting up a website of our own—friendsoftaylor.com—Fawley removed Taylor's pictures from his site. My brother Jeffrey told me that Fawley was clearly involved, and that he was already trying to distance himself from Taylor.

I tried not to think about it. I worked with Michael Smith, my colleague, on setting up Taylor's site. We posted a copy of the flyer, along with other pertinent information—age, date of disappearance, and so on—and photographs of Taylor and of the car. We urged people to contact the police hotline if they knew anything, and Michael set up a Paypal account for anyone who might want to donate money for a reward, or to help defray some of my mounting expenses.

Within hours, we started receiving donations. Frankly, I was stunned. I hadn't realized that people across the country were actually following the case, and I had not expected that kind of generosity. Every time a donation came in, no matter how modest, somebody in the room would do a little dance. We called it our Appreciation Dance, and it consisted mostly of mindless spinning and of equally mindless leg kicking, punctuated by shouts of *Woo hoo!* It was pretty silly, but it was exactly what we needed to help break the tension.

Many of the donations included notes of encouragement. People told us to remain optimistic, and to never give up hope. I was urged to believe that Taylor was fine and that she would be found, and I was told to pray for her safe return.

The next day, I began to get cards and letters at the hotel. Someone had discovered that I was staying at the Marriot, and the word got out, and people across the country were taking the time to write. Again, they told me they were thinking of me, and of Taylor, and praying for a positive outcome. I was deeply and genuinely moved. I had never imagined that something like this could make a difference, but it made all the difference in the world. Knowing that there were hundreds of people out there, praying for my little girl, was truly comforting.

On September 17, a Saturday, I was doing a live television interview when I noticed George taking a call on his cell phone. When the interview was over, George took me aside and told me that Taylor's car had been found. We called the police, and they told us that it had been found early that morning, by an off-duty police officer who had been walking his dog. The car was parked in a residential community near a church, less than two miles from

Taylor's dorm, and the Virginia license plates had been removed and replaced with stolen Ohio plates. The police had spent much of the day watching the car, hoping that someone would show up and try to drive away. After twelve hours, no one had appeared, so they impounded the car, used trained dogs to search the area, and called the FBI for help with the forensic investigation. So far, they had no leads, but this didn't trouble me at all. On the contrary: It had been twelve days since I'd received that early morning phone call telling me that Taylor was missing, and for the first time I entertained the vague hope that she would be found alive.

_____

5

PERSON OF INTEREST

After the police shared the news with us, they gave the story to the press and I was immediately deluged with interview requests. The next day, one of the reporters described me as "euphoric." I wouldn't say I was euphoric, but I was certainly more optimistic, and that's what I told reporters the next day: "It does make me a little more hopeful that she is alive."

I had wanted to go to the location, but Chief Monroe asked me to stay put. There were a number of detectives on the scene, he explained, interviewing people in the neighborhood, and a K-9 team was still out there, trying to track Taylor's scent. My presence would only create more confusion, he said, and that's the last thing he needed.

At that point, Chief Monroe had eleven people working on the case, and the task force included members of the FBI, the Virginia State Police, the campus police, and the Virginia Attorney

General's Office. He was doing everything in his power to find Taylor, and I respected his wishes and returned to the hotel to wait for his call.

Meanwhile, a number of my friends and family, including Matt, had heard the news and rushed to the site, but they were of course turned away. The police were determined not to let anyone contaminate the scene, and they made no exceptions—not even for Matt. As a result, Matt was very upset by the time he got back to the hotel, and he demanded to know why I hadn't called him the moment I heard about the car. I don't know what George told him, but they argued, and the argument escalated, and finally Ann intervened and asked them both to please calm down. Matt then proceeded to turn his rage on me, saying, "This is turning into *The Janet Show!*"

I was pretty furious myself at this point, and I shouted at him: "I don't have to listen to your shit anymore! Get the fuck out of my room!"

Matt left, but I was still furious with him. I was really pining for Taylor, and that brief moment of optimism gave way, once again, to the unthinkable. *What if she's dead?* I asked myself. *What if I never see her again?*

I began to blame Matt for everything. I began to think that none of this would be happening if he'd been a half-decent father. I know now that these thoughts came from a place of rage and anger, but I don't believe that makes them any less valid. A father's love is incredibly important to a child, especially to a young girl. A woman's sense of self-confidence and self-respect comes in large part from her interaction with her father, the dominant male figure in her life. Those critical early years are all about laying a solid foundation, and as I looked back I wondered if Matt couldn't have done more. I'm not suggesting he was entirely to blame, only that he could have done better. I'm sure I could have done better, too, because I know I'm not perfect, but at that moment I wasn't thinking about my own short-comings. I was thinking about how much I missed my little girl, and how worried I was, and instead of falling into a bottomless black hole of depression I decided to get pissed—and I had plenty of reasons to be pissed at Matt.

My room was still full of people, but suddenly I wanted to be alone. I was told that there was going to be a report about Taylor's car on *America's Most Wanted*, but I didn't want to see or hear it. I was physically and emotionally exhausted and very much at the end of my rope. I asked everyone to please leave and collapsed on the bed.

I couldn't sleep, though. I drifted in and out of consciousness, wondering what the police were up to, and hoping and praying for good news. In the morning, I was out of bed before anyone else, scouring the newspapers and flipping through the local television channels to see what I could find. "This is a tremendous break," Chief Monroe told reporters. "Now we can try to determine how long the car has been there and whether or not anyone may have seen the car being parked."

Another expert, Clint Van Zandt, a former FBI man, put it this way: "If somebody drove her car other than her, you have to re-adjust your rearview mirror. You have to move the seat back and forth. You've got . . . a rich supply of latent fingerprints . . . inside that car. You've got hairs and fibers."

I didn't know what to think. The idea that her car had been moved by other people made me wonder who might have done this to my daughter. I thought of Ben Fawley, and I wondered if he was involved, and whether he had acted alone. I tried not to think about the things that had been taken from his apartment—whips and chains, a machete, a hatchet—but I couldn't help it. I spent the better part of the day trying not to think at all, and waiting for developments that didn't come.

I don't remember going to bed that night, and I don't remember getting out of bed the following morning. All I remember is that it took all my strength to try to function like a normal person. It was almost as if I had to force my mind to get my body to do everything I had once taken for granted. *Okay, left foot in front of right foot. Now right foot. Pick up toothbrush. Brush teeth.*

Later that morning, we got word that one of the police dogs, a bloodhound, had picked up a scent. We weren't given any details, but Chief Monroe described it as a "successful track." He said he and his men were pursuing several leads, and we heard a rumor that they were talking to the occupants of a home that was a short distance from where the car had been found. By afternoon, more details began to emerge. The house was on Sheppard Street, and the police had talked to the young nephew of the couple who lived there. Apparently he had been at a party the previous night, and they hadn't connected with him till early that morning, but they had since picked him up for questioning. They subjected him to a polygraph test and word leaked out that he had failed two of the questions—specifically, that he didn't know Taylor, and that he'd never been in her car. The police held him for several hours, but then let him go.

I didn't know what to think. Much of this was hearsay, so it was hard to separate fact from fiction, but I was told the young man in question was friendly with the son of the cook at the Village Café. I didn't know if there was any truth to this, but it disturbed me deeply. I remembered what I'd been told about the way the cook had rubbed his hands with glee when Taylor's name had come up, and the way he had mouthed the words: *I love her.*

The next day, the paper said that thirty-seven sets of finger-prints had been found in the car. There was, however, no evidence of foul play.

On Monday, September 19, a candlelight vigil was held at Monroe Park, across from Taylor's dorm. I felt so emotionally fragile that I asked my cousin, Mike Davis, to go on my behalf. More than a hundred people turned up, including the Reverend Joseph P. Ellison, from the Essex Village Community Church, and they began with songs and prayers. Mike thanked everyone for coming, and asked them to please keep looking. "Help us find Taylor," he said. "If one of you was missing, Taylor was the kind of girl who would be out here tonight—she was a person who always reached out to help others."

When Mike got back to the hotel, he told me that he had been very moved by the show of support. Taylor had been at VCU for barely two weeks, but she had already touched countless lives.

"I know I should have gone," I said. "But I couldn't. In my mind, I associate vigils with death."

"That's not the way it was at all," he protested.

"I know," I said. "But I can't help it. That's what I'm thinking."

The next day, September 20, Chief Monroe called to tell me that they were going to bring Ben Fawley in for questioning as a "person of interest." He said he couldn't go into detail, but that he had wanted to share the news with me before the story broke in the press.

Within hours, the story was out. One of the papers reported that Fawley had seen Taylor barely an hour before she disappeared, but that he claimed not to have had any contact with her since. This was subsequently confirmed by Chris Collins, the criminal defense attorney who was representing Fawley. Collins further noted that Fawley had been interviewed at length, and that he had even been willing to take a lie-detector test, but that he, Collins, had asked him not to do so. By day's end, the police reiterated that Fawley was not a suspect in Taylor's disappearance. "At this time, the Richmond Police Department has not identified a suspect, but we have several persons of interest. We've interviewed several people extensively."

If this was true, it was news to me. I didn't know of anyone else who had been questioned in connection with Taylor's disappearance. All I knew was that too much time had elapsed since that first call from the campus police, back on September 7, and that with every passing day I had less reason to be optimistic.

I began to think, again, that we were never going to find her alive.

The next day, September 20, Matt appeared on Fox's *On the Record*, with Greta Van Susteren. This is a partial transcript of that appearance. It has been edited for clarity:

VAN SUSTEREN: Your daughter is supposed to be at college tonight.

BEHL: That's right—should be in class.

VAN SUSTEREN: Tough, isn't it? I mean, it's unthinkable what parents have to go through on this.

BEHL: Very tough.

VAN SUSTEREN: When did you last speak to your daughter?

BEHL: The day she left for Labor Day, the day she turned up missing, I saw her at about 4:30 in the afternoon at my home in Springfield.

VAN SUSTEREN: So, she was leaving the Northern Virginia area headed back to school?

BEHL: Correct.

VAN SUSTEREN: She give you any idea what she was going to do that evening or plans?

BEHL: No. She called me about twenty minutes of seven and let me know that she arrived at school safely and that there, you know, she basically didn't have any problems so that was it.

VAN SUSTEREN: So you never heard from her the rest of the evening or into the next day until you received a phone call from Janet about 5:00 a.m. Wednesday?

BEHL: Wednesday, right.

VAN SUSTEREN: Where did she usually park her car do you have any idea?

BEHL: She parked it over by an acquaintance of hers from Madison High School where she graduated from over on Marshall, pretty close to the intersection of Hancock and

Marshall across the street from the VCU police substation that's located there.

VAN SUSTEREN: All right, so that's near Ben Fawley's house coincidentally.

BEHL: Right around the corner.

VAN SUSTEREN: And that's about a mile and a half from where her car was discovered at least.

BEHL: Yes. Yes.

VAN SUSTEREN: All right. And you don't know that she did it for sure but that's usually where she parked her car?

BEHL: She parked it there all the time because she didn't have to pay for parking there.

VAN SUSTEREN: You've met Ben Fawley?

BEHL: Yes, I have.

VAN SUSTEREN: When did you first meet him?

BEHL: Early February, when Taylor was interested in going to VCU. I ended up taking her down there to spend the night at that house and go with her friend from high school to classes the next day and to the student union to eat, things like that.

VAN SUSTEREN: All right, your impression of him, I mean which may be favorable or unfavorable? It doesn't necessarily mean he had anything to do with her disappearance but I'm curious what did you think about him?

BEHL: At first I didn't know at that time, of course, that he was thirty-eight years old. I honestly thought he was probably mid- to late twenties. He was a little different with greenish hair and different colors in his hair but very personable to me, shook my hand, invited me into the house with Taylor, told me that the boy that she was going to see down there and his girlfriend would be back. . . . I didn't have any apprehensions at that time of, you know, letting Taylor be there, you know. I look at it from a standpoint that in a few months she was going to be going to college there anyway and I didn't see anything wrong. Nothing caused the hairs on the back of my neck to rise.

VAN SUSTEREN: Are you suspicious that he knows something about where your daughter is?

BEHL: I honestly don't know if he's telling everything. Certainly he knows something and whether he's told the police or not I don't know.

VAN SUSTEREN: Why do you think that? I mean it's conceivable that she walked to her car if she left her dorm room with the keys and she could have been nabbed by somebody else and never even made it to his house.

BEHL: Could have been, absolutely. I just don't know. It's just a very strange relationship.

VAN SUSTEREN: In what way?

BEHL: Thirty-eight-year-old man, seventeen-year-old girl, do the math.

VAN SUSTEREN: Any idea, I mean the stolen tags on the car or the car give—any clues in this car?

BEHL: Well, all of us are still waiting for the forensics information from the police, which has not been released yet.

VAN SUSTEREN: So how do you get through this?

BEHL: You just wake up every day and try to think about it and see what's coming up next. Some days are good. Some days are not so good. You go through euphoric highs like Saturday when they discovered the car thinking your daughter is coming home the next day and here we are four days, three days later and she's still not home.

The next day, Wednesday, September 21, I told the press that my family was offering an $11,000 reward for information about Taylor's disappearance. Some of that money had been collected from complete strangers through that Paypal account, but the bulk of it had come from family. Later in the day, I asked George to please go to Taylor's room and remove all of her personal belongings. When he was questioned about this by reporters he was very clear: "When Taylor comes home, it's not going to be to VCU."

I was asked later if this statement was meant as a criticism of the school, and I said nothing. But now I'm free to tell you: yes, it most definitely was. I did not feel then, nor do I feel today as I write this, that the campus police and the VCU administration moved quickly enough. They were slow to recognize the seriousness of the case, and even slower to acknowledge the fact that they needed help. Their whole investigation was marked by a lack of urgency. It took almost a week to convince them that Taylor was not a runaway, and several more days before they went to the Richmond Police Department for help. I am well aware that this would not have altered the outcome, but I continue to believe that things would have been resolved far more quickly if they hadn't been so determined to solve the crime without help.

My brother, Jeffrey, went to Taylor's dorm room with George to help remove Taylor's personal effects, and months later he wrote about the heart-breaking experience:

> One of the things that was so hard and seemed so not real for me was when Teenie asked me to go clean out Taylor's dorm room. Me not having attended college I had no idea what a dorm room life would be like. When I got into Taylor's room I saw what appeared to be a room not much bigger than a closet and I felt so bad that me, her uncle, was going through all of her personal belongings, just putting them hastily into cardboard boxes. I had recruited some help from some college kids to help carry some things down to the car. I again can remember thinking if there was some way I could change places with Taylor. It just didn't seem right having someone there stuffing your belongings into cardboard boxes. But this was a job that certainly was only for a direct family member.
>
> As I looked around Taylor's room, I saw things that Taylor liked. The pictures of the musicians that she liked, for example, and it seemed like just a bad dream that this was going on. . . . As bad as it seemed, all I could do was stuff her things in cardboard boxes since my wish of being able to trade places with her was in no way a possibility. It just needed to be done. But there was a teddy bear on top of her bunk that seemed to have a certain twinkle, and it seemed as if he just didn't want to go into a cardboard box. So I kept him aside and gave him to my sister.

The next day, VCU officials offered their own reward: $20,000 for any information that would lead to the return of my daughter. A cynic might say that this was a public relations ploy—their response to my criticism. All I can say is that the timing certainly seemed a little odd. In a written statement, VCU President Eugene P. Trani said, "Please keep Taylor, her family and friends in your thoughts as we hope for her safe return."

That same day, the *Richmond Times-Dispatch* carried a bizarre story about Fawley. Apparently Fawley had told police that a few hours after Taylor's disappearance, at around five in the morning, on September 6, he himself had been abducted by "unknown assailants." He said he had been walking through an alley near Franklin Street and Monument Avenue, at around 5:00 a.m., when he was "robbed by an unknown number of people." Fawley told police that his assailants put a bag over his head, hit him in the stomach, then shoved him into a car and drove to a remote location, where they dumped him by the side of a dirt road. I was flabbergasted. I read the story in complete disbelief. I thought that at any moment he would begin talking about aliens, the blinking lights on their spaceship, and the battery of tests he had been subjected to in his drug-induced, semiconscious state.

He told police that the assailants took about $400 worth of camera equipment and a small amount of cash, but he was a little fuzzy on the details. He explained that he'd had a few drinks earlier in the evening, and he suspected that they hadn't mixed well with the medication he was taking for a bipolar disorder. Bipolar disorder? The story got stranger as it went along. To say it lacked credibility, as one reporter noted, struck me as being the understatement of the year.

The next day, September 23, the police called to tell me that they were about to arrest Fawley. They warned me that the charges against him had nothing to do with Taylor's disappearance. I had to wait for the TV reports to find out exactly what they were charging him with, and those details didn't surface till later in the day. A TV crew was actually on hand to film the arrest. It took place at around three that afternoon, in the 400 block of Hancock Street, where I'd gone to speak to him two weeks earlier. A phalanx of armed officers descended on the building and several of them went inside and knocked on his door. Fawley emerged a few moments later, his hair and goatee dyed black. He was handcuffed and led away, looking as meek as a lamb.

Later in the day, more details emerged. It turned out that Fawley had been arrested on child pornography charges. Police had uncovered a cache of movies depicting adults and children in sexual acts. When I heard this, I felt sick. Chief Monroe was asked about the allegations. "Our investigation led to an individual that had possession of child pornography, which is of grave concern to us," he said. I assumed he was referring to the investigation into Taylor's disappearance, but he never said so specifically, and Fawley's lawyer, Chris Collins, did his best to downplay the connection, noting that the child pornography charges had nothing to do with Taylor. "They're investigating three people and they haven't ruled anybody out," he said. "They're just doing a really thorough job."

That night, I was interviewed by Ashley Wharton, who worked for the local NBC affiliate. I told her I had become almost physically ill when Fawley told police that he'd had a "personal relationship" with my daughter, but given what I'd learned from Taylor's friends I made no attempt to deny it. Still, I pointed out that Taylor was only seventeen, and that Fawley, a man twice her age, was certainly aware that he was committing a crime. "Maybe this was her dumb decision, but it is still wrong—it is still against the law," I said. "He's a sick man for doing it." At the same time, I tried to impress on her that I didn't give a damn about Fawley. "I'm glad that he is behind bars, but it doesn't help the police find Taylor. So, okay, he's arrested . . . but now I want to find my daughter. That is my ultimate goal."

Around this time, reporters began making obtuse references to Taylor's online life, and even quoting from her jottings on MySpace.com. At that point, I hadn't looked at the site. As I said earlier, I knew it existed, but I felt that by reading it I would somehow be violating my daughter's privacy. I guess I was a little naïve. I didn't realize at the time that these postings were very public, and that they were open to her friends and to friends of her friends— basically, to people she had never met.

On Monday, September 26, I appeared on CBS's *The Early Show* with Chief Monroe. I had been in Richmond for three weeks. "I'm trying not to think about how—what situation she could be in. I try not to feel, and just hope that if she can hear me—come home. You know? If they'll just let her walk away and just come on home." I also said I hoped Fawley would share what he knew with the police, and maybe help us find Taylor.

In all honesty, however, I must tell you that I thought Taylor was dead. I didn't want to believe it, though, and a very small part of me still had hope. But even if I had no hope, I didn't want everyone else to stop hoping. I wanted them to keep looking.

Chief Monroe told *The Early Show* that the task force was "just pushing along. Every day, there are a number of things we have to follow up on. There is an enormous amount of evidence that we've collected, both from Taylor's car and from the search warrants that we issued on Friday. It's a matter of linking any evidence that we have recovered to any information that we have in our possession or may have in our possession in the future." Asked if Fawley was considered a suspect, he said, "We don't know that yet. Quite naturally, he's one of only a few people that had contact with Taylor in the preceding twenty-four hours of her disappearance. He admitted to the fact that he was with her the night of her disappearance. So quite naturally, whatever information he could provide could be of great value to us."

That same day, Fawley appeared in court for a hearing on the child pornography charges. The judge was told that more than two dozen movie files were found on his computers, and that some depicted sex acts with children that looked to be barely one or two years old. Other files featured children between the ages of ten and fourteen. The judge further learned that Fawley was unemployed and lived off a monthly Social Security disability check because he suffered from a bipolar disorder. He was denied bond. There was no mention of Taylor, and no mention of his possible connection to her disappearance, but everyone knew that he was still the prime suspect.

When reporters came by the hotel after the hearing, looking for my reaction, I tried to focus on the only thing that mattered to me. "If he knows anything about Taylor or where she is, maybe he'll share it," I said. And on the off-chance that he had nothing to do with her disappearance, I appealed to the public at large: "Whoever has her, let her walk away. Let her come home. I need my baby, and I want her back."

That night, Marilyn Bardsley, a reporter with Court TV, aired a report of her own. This is an excerpt from that report: "Young Taylor did do a few things that put her at risk. High on that list is her relationship with Ben Fawley, a man more than twice her age with a criminal past who is now in jail on child pornography charges. Also, she was walking around in an urban area, presumably unescorted, at 10:30 at night. Finally, at least some of her new friends in Richmond were people who were very much involved in the local drug scene."

I found the report offensive. For one thing, Marilyn Bardsley didn't know Taylor, and she was implicating her in the drug scene by association. I wondered who her sources were, and why she didn't name them. I knew Taylor. She may have had friends who experimented with drugs, but I was pretty sure Taylor didn't do them. The other thing I didn't understand was this business about walking around the campus *without an escort*. What did that mean? The VCU police department had more than seventy officers on its staff, making it one of the largest campus police forces in the country. Shouldn't Taylor have felt safe on her own campus?

As much as her report upset me, I did my best to keep track of anything related to Taylor, no matter how marginal it might appear. With the help of family and friends, we kept on top of everything—television, newspapers, radio reports, magazines. I was hoping that I would see or hear something that everyone else had missed—a crucial clue that would lead us to her.

At that stage, however, the media didn't have much more to say about Taylor, and they were focused on Ben Fawley. A more complete picture of him began to emerge, and as the details trickled in I realized that he was a lot more broken than Taylor had ever imagined. He was from Doylestown, Pennsylvania, estranged from his immediate family, and had two children of his own. He also had an impressive criminal record. There were arrests for car theft, and for assault—two assaults against women, and another three on members of his own family. There were charges for disorderly conduct and reckless endangerment going back to 1986, some of which resulted in convictions. Several reporters took the time to look through Fawley's website, where he described himself as a "Goth/Skater from the 1980s." He explained that the nickname "Skulz," was a result of his fascination with human skulls, which he drew and collected. I also learned that Fawley had worked at the university's two recreation centers, handing out towels and checking ID cards. He apparently held the jobs between April 2001 and January 2003. I didn't understand it. Why would the university give a convicted felon that kind of unfettered access to its young students? It sickened me.

Other details were sketchy. The bipolar disorder was described as "severe" by his lawyer, and there were rumors that he'd had a rough childhood. I didn't know what kind of childhood he'd had, but that didn't condone anything. On the contrary, I was disgusted by his checkered history. Here was a man who had been getting in trouble for almost twenty years and had never been held accountable for any of it.

On the heels of these discoveries, and without any warning whatsoever, I learned from a press report that Ben Fawley was no longer a "person of interest." According to the report, the police interviewed Fawley at great length and concluded that he was not relevant to the case. As I was struggling to process what this meant, the phone rang. Chief Monroe was on the other end. "I'm just calling to tell you that despite what you've heard this doesn't make him any less of a suspect," he said. "We're only doing this for legal and political reasons. I don't want you to worry." He also suggested that it might be time for me to go home. I thought about that. I'd been living at the Marriot for three weeks, and there wasn't really anything left for me to do in Richmond. Plus Chief Monroe was running the task force, so I knew I was in good hands.

"You're probably right," I said.

"I know I'm right," he replied.

Ann and Mike concurred. They had been by my side since my first full day in Richmond, and they could see it was taking its toll. It was taking a toll on them, too.

I called my friend Cindi White, in Sterling Park, Virginia, and asked if she would come down to take me home. She and her husband, Jamey, arrived the next day. I would make the trip home with her, and he would drive my car back to Vienna.

For a while, I entertained the idea of sneaking away, so that the press wouldn't make a big fuss, or read something into it, but I'd been at the Marriot so long, and been treated so kindly by the staff, that I couldn't leave without saying good-bye. I spent the better part of an hour looking for everyone who had gone out of their way for me, and thanking them for their attentiveness and generosity. I also gave each of them gift cards from World Cup II, a local coffee shop. The coffee shop had donated several hundred dollars worth of coffee during the long, fruitless search for Taylor, and this was my way of thanking them, and of thanking the staff at the Marriot. As it turned out, the World Cup management refused to let me pay for the gift cards, and I still haven't figured out how to acknowledge their generosity—so I'm doing it here.

On the drive back to Vienna, Cindi and I talked about her sister Toni, who had been married to my brother, Bo. She'd been in a terrible car wreck years earlier, and the accident took the life of their twenty-two-year-old son, William, our nephew. Toni herself had been severely injured, and spent several weeks in the hospital, followed by three months at the home of her parents, where she continued to recuperate. It was Cindi who had finally taken Toni back to her house, and she told me that she would never forget the way Toni had fallen apart when they returned. "It was incredibly traumatic," Cindi said. "That was the house she had shared with William, and the moment she stepped through the front door she realized that she would never see him again."

In a way, I was preparing myself for a similar experience, and that was the reason I'd called Cindi to come for me in Richmond. I wanted someone at my side who understood what it was going to be like. I was returning to the house I'd shared with my daughter, and I was trying to come to terms with the fact that Taylor would probably not be coming home again. Not soon, not ever. Still, I wasn't completely sure. Somewhere deep down, I had a tiny bit of hope, and my hope gave me strength. It wasn't much, but it's what I needed to get me through the front door.

When I walked into the house, the first thing I saw was a huge flower arrangement. It was from Madison Shell, my local gas station. The day that Taylor and I had left for VCU, we stopped for gas, and our friend Frank had come out to talk to us. Taylor and I had known Frank for several years, and he was so excited for Taylor you would have thought she was his own daughter. He told her to behave herself at college, and to study hard, and to come back and see him whenever she was in the neighborhood. Taylor gave him a little hug before we left.

The second thing I saw was a literal mountain of mail on the kitchen counter. I went over and sifted through the pile, hundreds and hundreds of letters, most of them from complete strangers. Some of them were addressed directly to me, others were more pointed: *To Taylor's Mother,* for example. Or, *To The Family of Taylor Behl.* I opened two or three and glanced at them. Complete strangers were writing to tell me they were praying for me, and for Taylor. One woman had even included her phone number, and she urged me to call if I needed anything. It was both overwhelming and heartwarming, and I found myself fighting tears.

Everything else in the house was exactly as I had left it on the morning of September 7, including the two cats. And everything that belonged to Taylor was exactly as she had left it. I looked around, feeling numb. My home felt oddly surreal. I felt as if I was watching this happening to another version of me—a diminished version of my real self. I didn't understand it. Either my mind was playing tricks on me or the anti-depressants were doing strange things to my perception.

Cindi spent the night with me, and in the morning, when she left for work, other friends came over to stand watch. By the third night, however, I decided I wanted to be alone. I had been surrounded by people for more than three weeks, twenty-four hours a day, seven days a week, and I couldn't have survived without their help and support, but I thought it was time to begin to process everything that had happened and was still happening. I wanted to think about Taylor. I wanted to think about everything we did during her last weekend home. I wanted to remember the way she beamed when she went up to get her high school diploma, and of the way she'd looked during the graduation party we'd had in our little yard.

I was tired. I felt as if I'd been in the ring for three weeks, fighting with the campus police, fighting with the university, fighting to get the media's attention, fighting with Taylor's father, and fighting to suppress the feelings that had been threatening to overwhelm me from the moment I'd received that horrific, early-morning phone call.

On my first night alone, I took a sleeping pill. In the morning, I tried to keep busy by tending to manageable, mundane tasks. I balanced my checkbook. I answered e-mail. I went though a few cards and letters and answered those, too. I made some inquiries about the house in Roanoke, which I'd recently purchased, and I called my boss at work to discuss the future. She told me I needed to make a decision about the job, noting that I had four options: One, I could return to work. Two, I could ask for an extended emergency leave. Three, I could quit. And four, I could let them fire me. The most appealing option seemed to be the last one. If they fired me, I wouldn't lose my medical benefits, but if I quit I'd have nothing. Unemployment compensation wasn't even an issue because I had no intention of looking for a job. I already had a full-time job, and that job was to find my daughter.

I honestly didn't know what to do, and I didn't want to think about the future, immediate or otherwise. All I knew was that I wanted my mind to stop racing, so I sat down in front of my computer and spent two hours playing Zuma, an absolutely mindless game involving a frog and bouncing balls of various colors. For two hours, I only thought about the frog and the bouncing balls, then I took another sleeping pill and went to bed.

The next day, September 30, my boss called again. She wanted to know if I'd made a decision, and I told her I had. "Lay me off," I said. And that's what she did. Later that same day, as if to soften the blow, I got a call from one of the owners of Jammin' Java. They told me that George had called to discuss the possibility of holding a benefit concert for Taylor, and that they wanted to hold it that very Sunday. They said I could do whatever I wanted with the money they managed to raise: Add it to the reward. Pay my bills. Buy groceries.

The next day, while volunteers ran around town collecting donations from local businesses, Cindi and I had flyers made up: Taylor's smiling face, along with details about the coming benefit, and ran around town passing them out and putting them up in store windows. Everyone was incredibly nice, except for the manager of one store, who was so rude that Cindi got into a huge, screaming fight with him. "I can't believe you are so insensitive! This is that woman's daughter!" He tried to back pedal. "You didn't tell me it was *her* daughter!" And I turned to him and said, "It doesn't matter whose daughter it is. It's somebody's daughter, and she's missing. That is the wrong attitude. You have just lost my business forever."

But honestly, that was the only unpleasant experience. Everyone else was generous and thoughtful, and I felt as if the entire community was really pulling for me.

The boys at Jammin' Java did an amazing job. Steve Buckhantz, a local sportscaster and good friend, was Master of Ceremonies, and three bands volunteered their time. The event was a huge success. People kept coming by with checks and cash and with words of encouragement. *Don't give up. Have faith. We're praying for Taylor to come home.*

Steve Shannon, our local delegate, stopped by and made a speech about missing and exploited children, and there were a number of reporters on hand, all of whom interviewed me and even wished me well.

When it was all over, we had collected eight thousand dollars. I was so moved I almost wept. "I don't know how to thank you guys," I said.

"We just want you to know that we love Taylor, and that we're here for you if you need anything."

I didn't cry—I was still refusing to cry in public—but I could feel the blood rushing to the back of my throat.

The next day, October 3, an article appeared in the *Washington Post*. It was written by Jamie Stockwell, and it opened as follows:

Before she disappeared from a Richmond university four weeks ago, Taylor Marie Behl recorded her moods, her crushes, her insecurities in fifty entries she posted online over the span of twelve months. In language both spare and pensive, she detailed rites of passage, from earning her driver's license to preparing for university.

With her chronicles, Behl, 17, of Vienna gained entry into a vast virtual community, a very public arena in which her writings were there for anyone to see at any time, a personal diary with no key.

Now police also are privy to the disagreements that Behl had with her parents, her emotions on any given day, even her sexual exploits.

The article quoted from Taylor's online musings, and I learned that her very first entry made reference to an argument I'd had with her when a boy visited the house while I was out. "I'm just trouble," Taylor had written.

I immediately remembered the incident. I arrived home one afternoon and saw this kid running out the back door. I was mad. Taylor was not allowed to have guys in the house when I wasn't there, and she'd never done it before (not that I knew of, anyway). I looked at Taylor, fuming, and at the boy's glasses, sitting on the coffee table, and I remember wondering, *Do they think I'm stupid? His glasses are on the coffee table!*

"Hello!" I said finally. "We have rules in this house! Since when did you get sneaky on me?" I didn't make a big fuss, though, because I'm not a fan of arguing, and before long the boy came crawling back like a thief. He wasn't tall enough to get over the rear fence, and he needed his glasses. He apologized, and Taylor apologized, and after he left Taylor apologized once more and assured me that it wouldn't happen again. The whole thing had been quietly forgotten, until now—until I found myself reading about this minor domestic incident in a national newspaper.

There were many other entries in Taylor's website log, or blog, and I read them with caution.

Stockwell wrote:

Mostly, Behl's online writings captured the angst and mood swings typical among teenagers.

There were moments of sadness: "I now know that everyone is useless and really doesn't care."

There were moments of anger: "I'm so [expletive] tired of everyone making decisions in my best interest. Don't I get a [expletive] say? NO. Sorry, not 'til you're 18."

And there were moments of utter and exposed joy: "I'll have my own car on Sunday . . . yessssssssssssssss!"

The thrust of the article, however, dealt with the risks of posting one's innermost thoughts and secrets on websites. A blog was basically an online diary. It was a way for people—mostly young—to create a social network in cyberspace. As they searched for new friendships and new connections, they could tell the world about themselves—often in intimate detail. But it wasn't just friends who were watching. There were predators out there, lying in wait, setting traps, looking into the hearts and minds of these unsuspecting kids.

When I'd been in Richmond, several reporters had tried to suggest that Taylor had been a victim of cyberspace. This might have made a good story, but it wasn't accurate. She hadn't met Ben Fawley online. She'd met him in person. On the other hand, the relationship may have evolved in cyberspace, so it's possible that Fawley used that to his advantage.

After reading Stockwell's article, I took a closer look at Taylor's profile. I was wary, and I felt as if I were tiptoeing through her various entries, worrying about what I might find. I wondered, for example, why she used the online name Bitter. Taylor was many things, but bitter was not one of them. Maybe she was trying to create an online persona that had nothing to do with who she was. Maybe that was the appeal of cyberspace—you could become somebody else.

There was, as Stockwell noted, the usual teenage angst: Missing her friends. Wanting more friends. Being moody. None of these were particularly troubling, but a short time later I came across an entry that *did* bother me. She had written it in late March 2005, and it referred to an incident that had taken place at her father's house. She was spending the weekend there, per the custody arrangement, with Matt and his live-in girlfriend, and the girlfriend's son had hit on her:

> I don't really want to be here. I want to be home in my bed where
> I know I'm safe. I would be home alone, except for the cats, and
> I'm fine with that. My dad's g/f's son is creepy, he hits on me and
> it makes me very uncomfortable.

I already knew about this because she had told me about it, and it had happened more than once. In fact, on one occasion, Glynnis had gone to visit Taylor at Matt's house, and the boy hit on both of them and offered them liquor. Taylor later admitted that she'd had a wine cooler, but she said that nothing untoward had happened.

I had gotten pretty mad, but not at Taylor. I was mad at the boy, for obvious reasons—he was over twenty-one and should have known better—and I was mad at Matt, for his complete lack of awareness. I didn't want my daughter spending the night in a house with such limited supervision, and I had called Matt to rail at him and tell him that I wasn't going to let Taylor visit anymore. "You do that," he said, "and you can forget about child support."

I went to talk to a lawyer, and I took Taylor with me. Taylor told the lawyer what she had told me, saying she had to deal with the same unpleasantness every time she went to Matt's house. But she also said that she was worried about alienating Matt. She was leaving for college soon, and he had already agreed to pay her tuition, and she didn't want to do anything to jeopardize that.

"I think the environment your father is providing is unacceptable on several levels," the lawyer said. "But you're almost eighteen. As soon as you turn eighteen, you can make your own decisions about whether you want to spend the night under his roof. Meanwhile, I think you should try to make him aware of what's going on, and of how much it's bothering you."

When Taylor told her father about the most recent incident, he had her move her things into the bedroom closest to his. It wasn't much, but it was something, and Taylor seemed okay with it. Of course, there was another entry that explained why she was okay with it.

Under THREE THINGS THAT SCARE YOU, Taylor had written:

001. Boys

002. Men

003. My dad

It bothered me that she was afraid of her father. No child should be afraid of her father.

There were other entries. Under WHO I'D LIKE TO MEET, Taylor had written, "Someone who is kind." I wondered if someone had been unkind to her, and my first thought was that I would hunt the bastard down and kill him.

Under THREE THINGS YOU WANT TO DO BEFORE YOU DIE, she had written:

001. be happy

002. make a difference in someone's life

003. find real love

There were also entries that showed another, lighter side of Taylor. Under THREE CAREERS YOU'RE CONSIDERING, she had written:

001. Trophy wife

002. shop owner

003. bum

And when asked what her coworkers thought of her, she replied with great confidence: "You have what it takes to rule the world." I agreed with her wholeheartedly. "You do have what it takes to rule the world, honey," I thought. "No doubt about it."

The day after Jamie Stockwell's article appeared in the *Washington Post*, the authorities in Richmond got their first big break in the case. Erin Crabill, an ex-girlfriend of Fawley's, had been shown some of Fawley's personal photographs, on his website, and she recognized a house that Fawley had once taken her to. It was about seventy-five miles east of Richmond, near the home of Erin's parents.

The following day, October 5, the police called my cousin, Ann Martin. They told her they had searched the property and found a body. It was in a shallow ravine, not far from a dirt road. They told Ann that they were on their way to Vienna, to talk to me, and they asked her to meet them at my house. They didn't want me to be alone when they shared the news with me.

I knew none of this. Ann called and said she was in the neighborhood and wanted to stop by, and I knew immediately that she was lying. Ann worked in an office. She didn't drive around my neighborhood in the middle of the day.

"Okay," I said. "Come on over."

I told her that I was going to take a shower, and said I would leave the front door unlocked, then I called my friend Cindi, and asked her to please come over. I didn't explain anything—I guess the emotion in my voice said enough.

The moment I got in the shower, I began to cry. My whole body was convulsed by sobs. I knew what was coming, and for the life of me—for the life of Taylor—I did not want to face it.

I was in the shower for more than half an hour. I knew Ann and Cindi were downstairs, waiting for me, and I knew they had bad news. Finally I realized I couldn't put it off any longer. I got out and dried myself and got dressed—I have trouble getting out of the shower to this day—and went downstairs.

Ann and Cindi were waiting for me in the living room. A split-second after I walked inside, the doorbell rang. I hadn't even had time to say hello. Ann went and got the door and two police officers walked inside. I could tell from the expressions on their faces that they were there with the worst possible news. For an entire month, I'd been hoping and praying that this day would never come, but the day was here—the wait was over.

I sat down. One of the officers told me that Erin, the ex-girlfriend, had recognized the location from a photograph, and that one of the campus police officers had driven out to the site with her to take a look. When they found a body, members of the task force flew to the scene in a helicopter, and they all seemed to think it might be Taylor.

"Why do you think it's Taylor?" I asked. "Did you see her diamond earring? The stud in her nose?" I didn't realize it at the time, but those questions were incredibly naïve. The body had been out in the elements for a month. What did I think was left?

Both officers looked down at their feet. "The black hoodie was there," one of them said.

I couldn't breathe. I sat there, not breathing. I felt that if I moved, I would break into a million pieces.

"We're sorry about this, ma'am," the other officer said. I didn't look up at him, but I could tell by the way his voice cracked that he was truly sorry. After another moment of silence, he added, "We're going to need dental records to make a positive identification."

Nothing in the world prepares you for that. The police were in my house, asking for dental records so that they could identify a body they believed to be my daughter's.

I looked at my cousin Ann, then at Cindi, then at the police officers. Those two men had never even met Taylor, but the pain in their faces was so intense that I wanted to comfort them. But I couldn't move—I could hardly breathe.

"I'll call her dentist," I said.

"If you would authorize it, ma'am, and give us his address, we'll stop by and pick the records up ourselves."

I don't remember exactly what happened next. I gave the officers the address, and I think Ann walked them to the door and let them out, and then I called the dentist, Bobby Sears, a long-time friend. When I told him that two police officers were on their way over, he began to cry.

I remember sitting there for a long time, staring at my hands, clasped together in my lap, and wondering how I would feel when I found out that Taylor was never coming home. I couldn't even *imagine* what that would be like—to know that my baby girl was gone. Gone forever. And I still can't imagine it. Because even now as I write this, I don't believe it—I can't accept it.

Any moment now, I tell myself. *Any moment now Taylor's going to come walking through that front door. Any moment now, my baby girl is coming home.*

6.

___

FOREVER GONE

After the police left, it was just Ann and Cindi and me in the house, with that big, oppressive emptiness. None of us was crying. I knew that if I started crying I'd never stop, and Cindi and Ann knew that they had to be strong for me, as they had been from the start.

"You okay?" Ann asked.

"No," I said.

It was odd, sitting there, actively *not* feeling. I couldn't allow myself to feel. That was the only way to get through this. For an entire month, I'd been dreading that visit from the cops, and now they'd come and gone, but I refused to let it register. I was just going to keep moving forward as if none of this was happening.

I picked up the phone and called my mother, who had already returned to South Carolina. I suggested that she come back up for the weekend, but I didn't go into detail. "We'll go to Famous Dave's for that bread pudding you love," I said. I'm sure she suspected the worst, but she didn't ask, and I didn't volunteer anything.

The moment I hung up, the phone rang. It was a reporter. The media had been told about the body, and they wanted to know how I felt. *How I felt?* I had no idea how I felt. I didn't feel anything. I was standing on the edge of an abyss, and if I allowed myself to feel I would have toppled headlong into it.

I told the reporter I would get back to him, and I called George Peterson. He had just heard the news himself. He thought I should make a brief statement to reporters as soon as possible. If I didn't, they wouldn't stop hounding me. I asked him to arrange it, then I hung up and called my mother back. This time I told her about the two officers, and I went through everything they'd said. "Please come as soon as you can," I said. "And bring appropriate clothes."

She was devastated, but she held herself together for me. "Oh, Teen," she said, her voice cracking. "I'm so sorry."

"I know you are, Mom."

When I got off the phone, I called everyone in the family so that they wouldn't hear it first on the news. It was excruciating. I've never made so many people cry in such a short period of time. Every phone call released a fresh flood of tears.

Before long, George arrived at the house. He hugged me, and I felt strangely removed, as if I was having an out-of-body experience—watching from above as George hugged a woman who looked like me but wasn't really me at all.

"You okay?" he asked.

I nodded. Everyone always asks that—*You okay?*—when they know you're not anywhere goddamn near okay. But what else can they ask?

A few minutes later, the reporters began to arrive, congregating out front, and before long George asked me if I was ready.

"I guess so," I said.

George and Ann led me outside to face the press. I was exhausted—I was expending huge amounts of energy to keep myself from falling apart—and I must have sounded like an automaton. "I'm sure you can imagine the shock and horror I feel knowing that the body found is most likely my baby's," I said. It didn't feel like me or even sound like my voice. "My mind still cannot absorb the fact that someone could do something this cruel and heinous to my seventeen-year-old child. I am positive the authorities will bring these sub-humans to justice, and I pray they receive the death penalty. . . . My thanks and gratitude to everyone who helped in the search. . . . Whether it was time spent or money contributed, or—most comforting—your prayers, thank you from the bottom of my sad and broken heart."

I can't remember exactly what happened next, but I do remember telling Cindi that my mother was coming, and that we absolutely had to clean the house. We finished at ten o'clock that night, and I paused once, to cry, and I vaguely remember going up to bed.

In the morning, the house began to fill with friends and family, and I remember hugging people, and being hugged in return. I also remember trying to get a little food into my mouth, and I remember going back to bed—to escape into sleep yet again. Being awake didn't feel like being awake, anyway. I felt as if I were underwater. Everything was distorted, and when voices reached me they sounded muted and far away. I kept hearing the same words over and over again—*I'm so sorry, I'm so sorry, I'm so sorry*—and for the life of me I couldn't figure out why everyone was apologizing, or what they had done.

I also remember making a call to a funeral home, Money & King, right there in Vienna, so they could help me figure out what I was supposed to do next. The gentleman on the phone was incredibly kind, but even so I was overwhelmed by everything that lay ahead of me.

On October 6, the day before my birthday, the same two officers returned to the house to tell me that they had made a positive identification. I knew what they were going to tell me the moment I saw them at the front door, and I wondered why they had even bothered making the long drive. It seemed like a macabre formality. Why were they hammering away at me? Didn't they realize that this was already painful enough? I *knew*. Then again, did I? Maybe that's why they were there, because they had been through this before, with countless other people, and they knew something that I didn't know: That I wasn't really listening; that I didn't want to hear it.

"Thank you for coming by," I said.

"We're very sorry," they said.

"I know," I said.

The police then shared the story with the press, and it broke on the television news that night, and in the papers the following morning. Chief Monroe was quoted as saying that it was "not incorrect" to consider Fawley a suspect in Taylor's death. As far as I knew, this was the first time he had said so.

I was also told about a report on Court TV, filed, again, by Marilyn Bardsley, in which she interviewed a man who said he knew Taylor, and who described her as a "straight arrow" who was running with a "rough crowd." He also said that he had gone skateboarding with her a few times, and that he'd recently met Ben Fawley. He said he had been shocked to learn that Taylor had a personal relationship with Fawley. "It was like she was leading a second life," he said.

I found the whole story disturbing. I didn't understand why the man wanted to talk to the media, or why Bardsley would even bother interviewing him.

On the heels of this, George Peterson and I spoke with Fox News's Greta Van Susteren. Greta had become something of a friend to me. She called almost every day, just to check in, and she was always incredibly considerate. She was very upset at the start of the interview, and it took her a few moments to pull herself together.

This is a partial transcript of that appearance, edited for clarity:

VAN SUSTEREN: Now to Virginia, where Taylor Behl's loved ones have had their worst fears confirmed. Using dental records, police positively identified the body of the seventeen-year-old college freshman. Taylor's mother, Janet Pelasara, joins us live in Washington, along with her lawyer, George Peterson. Janet, I told you more than once, you know, how I feel and others feel. Viewers have written dozens and dozens of e-mails to express their condolences to you.

PELASARA: Thank you.

VAN SUSTEREN: Where do we begin?

PELASARA: It's the beginning of the true nightmare for me. I mean . . . the past four weeks have been just a blur, and reality is going to set in very shortly.

VAN SUSTEREN: You were notified yesterday that a body had been found. How is that done? I mean, do the police call you? Are they gentle about it?

PELASARA: They were very gentle. The Richmond police called my cousin and told her that the police were coming and for her to come to my house. And she called and said that she was in the neighborhood and would stop by. And so she was there for when the two officers came by to tell me that they had found a body in a shallow grave and they believed it to be Taylor, but they couldn't confirm it, and it wasn't to go out of, you know, this room. And three hours later, the media had it on the TV.

VAN SUSTEREN: Did they say why? Was it clothing, identification, anything that gave them a level of certainty?

PELASARA: Taylor's black sweatshirt, her black hoodie that she was last seen in, was there.

VAN SUSTEREN: And so then today, they gave the official word. The same procedure?

PELASARA: Yes. Yes. They came in, and the pain on the officers' faces were—you know, was sad for them. I know it was hard for them to come and tell me that. But they were, you know, very, very nice, very nice about it.

VAN SUSTEREN: I mean, it's pretty amazing, what this sort of joint task force—there's a different—the Richmond police, the FBI, even the VCU, I mean, there's been a bunch of police organizations looking for her, right?

PELASARA: Yes.

VAN SUSTEREN: I mean, they've done an unbelievable job considering, you know, the difficulty of it.

PELASARA: And it was actually the VCU police that was with Ben Fawley's ex-girlfriend that found her.

VAN SUSTEREN: And what was it? They looked at some photographs?

PELASARA: On Ben Fawley's website. They tried to identify each place, and the ex-girlfriend said, "Yes, I know where this picture was taken," and took them there.

VAN SUSTEREN: George, the investigation now, you know, goes in earnest. I mean, it's been going on, looking for Taylor, but now it goes to a new level. Have they told you, given you any idea of, you know—I mean, Ben Fawley's everyone's suspect. Have they indicated whether they think there are other people involved?

PETERSON: Not at present. I know that they are looking for a link between other people who may be involved, but I think that their prime person of interest or their prime suspect at this point is Ben Fawley.

VAN SUSTEREN: What about in terms of, you know, grand jury investigations going on?

PETERSON: I understand that there is a grand jury investigation going on. It actually met yesterday and had, I think, eight witnesses before it. And I understand it's going to convene again on October 19, where additional witnesses will appear.

VAN SUSTEREN: Ben Fawley has not been charged yet in the disappearance. We expect it, is that right, in the death of Taylor?

PETERSON: I certainly would expect it in the near future.

VAN SUSTEREN: Did the police say anything to you about that?

PETERSON: Not at present.

VAN SUSTEREN: Janet, did they say it to you? Do they say that Ben Fawley—I mean, I suspect him, and I think probably the rest of the nation does. But did the police officially say anything to you?

PELASARA: I believe they used the word "suspect."

VAN SUSTEREN: You know, it's hard to understand, you know, how you send a child off to college—and in fact, you saw her that day. She goes off, happily going off after her second week of school, and then not a month later, you're sitting here with me, talking about this.

PELASARA: Yes. And I still can't fully comprehend that Taylor's never coming home again.

VAN SUSTEREN: She's your only child?

PELASARA: Uh-huh.

VAN SUSTEREN: I don't know how you've gotten through this last month. You've been determined to find her. We've now, unfortunately, gotten in the position where you now have found her. So I mean, I know it was just today and yesterday that you've confronted this horrible reality. So what do you do? I mean, have you even thought about it? I mean, do you get involved with the investigation and keep pushing it?

PELASARA: No. I actually—just since I've been home from Richmond, I let them tell me, you know, what they're doing. I've, you know, looked at the photograph of things that they had taken out of Ben's house. I found a couple little pieces of paper where Taylor had written names and phone numbers. I sent them to the police so they could check it out. I made funeral arrangements today. They can take care of the investigation. I'm quite happy to only hear updates.

VAN SUSTEREN: Family from out of town here?

PELASARA: Yes.

VAN SUSTEREN: Everyone's gathered around?

PELASARA: They are starting today. My sister will be in on Saturday, and my brother will be here shortly.

VAN SUSTEREN: You must want to kill Ben Fawley.

PELASARA: If he is the person that did it, then I could feel like that.

VAN SUSTEREN: See, you get to know so many of these people, I mean, people who go through this hell, you know, Beth Holloway Twitty, Dave Holloway's going to join us later. I mean, you know, where they have children—we had a young woman, LaToyia Figueroa, in Philadelphia, where, you know, life seems to be going along rather joyously, and all of a sudden, everybody's life is ruined.

PELASARA: He'll get his.

VAN SUSTEREN: We later hear that Ben Fawley had said that he was kidnapped himself, the early morning hours of the sixth. And you smile.

PELASARA: Truly, when I was reading that article, I expected to read about aliens—you know, that aliens had abducted him. I mean, it's just total—I believe it's just total fabrication.

PETERSON: And I think, with that alibi, he's essentially established the timeline of when something happened to Taylor, the fact that he's picked out, 5:00 a.m. or 6:00 a.m. in the morning to suggest that he was kidnapped, and then, of course, he reports it twelve hours later. I think that's the timeline we're looking at.

VAN SUSTEREN: Well, I hope Taylor gets justice, and I hope you do, too, Janet.

PELASARA: Thank you.

VAN SUSTEREN: As well as the rest of her family because you know, we were all watching and hoping for a much different ending. Thank you, Janet.

Greta was genuinely sincere, as she had been all along. I know that at times it might have seemed as if she was in my face, but she was doing her job, and she was doing it as tactfully as she could. That helped me sit through it without falling apart—that and the fact that my emotions had gone into hibernation. As I'd told her, I still couldn't fully comprehend that Taylor was never coming home again.

Meanwhile, Matt was giving an interview to Nancy Grace, over on CNN. This is a partial transcript of that interview:

GRACE: I want to go straight out to a very special guest joining us tonight. Taylor's father is with us, Matt Behl. Sir, I sure am sorry.

BEHL: Thank you.

GRACE: Mr. Behl, this must have just been the worst day you could ever have imagined.

BEHL: It's a day that I never would have imagined would have happened. Parents don't outlive their kids.

GRACE: What has been going through your head since Taylor went missing?

BEHL: Just a bunch of different scenarios. Did she run off? Was she abducted by somebody? Is she being held against her will? Is she OK? Is she cold? It just—the range of emotions is just incredible. And there's so many things that occurred during the course of the month that she was gone, that, you know, when we—when they found her car in Richmond, you think the next day, they're going to find your child. When they convene a grand jury, you feel that you're going to get the answers that are going to bring your child home. Well, we got those answers, and it wasn't the one we were looking for.

GRACE: You know, I keep seeing pictures of Taylor. We're showing the video that your family had of her as a little girl, just so full of life. I was hoping against hope, weren't you, that Taylor was going to turn up, that this couldn't possibly be her, that somehow everything would be explained away?

BEHL: Yeah, you always hold that glimmer of hope, but I guess when there were so many things pointing to Mathews [county], the Mathews site where the body was found, and the investigation that the task force had done, that I think

that we were pretty resigned to the fact that that was probably going to be her.

On October 7, my birthday, I learned from Chief Monroe that
it might be weeks before charges were filed. This was not like an
episode of *Law & Order*. In real life, crimes weren't resolved in tidy,
forty-nine minute packages. Still, I wasn't as disturbed by this as I
might have been. The Richmond Police Department had my full
confidence, and I already knew that they had the right guy in custody. I was sure that by the time they were finished reviewing all
the evidence, forensic and otherwise, they would know what I already knew: that Ben Fawley had murdered my daughter. He
would never get out of prison. He would never again hurt anyone.

That same night, a Friday, there was a ceremony at VCU, at the
Student Commons. I didn't go because it was my birthday, and be-
cause my house was full of family and friends, and because I knew
Matt was going. I figured he could represent the family.

That was the saddest, most confusing birthday of my entire
life, and I'm sure it was equally surreal for my friends and family.
People kept coming by with trays of food, most of it home cooked,
standing around, whispering. Nobody knew how to act or what to
say. It felt exactly like a funeral—*my* funeral.

The next day, I heard that Matt had made a very nice speech
at the ceremony, thanking everyone who showed up, and thanking the police for their efforts. I also learned that the Dean of
Student Affairs addressed the crowd, and that he fell apart before
he could finish.

Matt appeared on *The Early Show* that day, Monday, October 10. He said we would be burying Taylor on Thursday, which would have been her eighteenth birthday. "Of course, this is something we had not planned," he said.

The interviewer then spoke about this whole business with websites, because this seemed to be a real source of fascination for the press, and for the public. Matt played along. "Children are putting out a lot of personal information about themselves," he said. "I don't think parents are wholly aware of it."

Taylor had not met Fawley on the Internet, and I had pointed this out repeatedly. They had been introduced by a mutual friend, and then had communicated through the Internet. Still, I understood the fascination. Cyberspace was a strange, new universe, and these kids found it very exciting, but it was obviously not without its dangers. I did not know much about the whole phenomenon before Taylor disappeared, but I was learning. In fact, while I'd been in Richmond looking for my daughter, I'd read a story about a fourteen-year-old girl who went off with a fifty-three-year-old man she met online. Since then, I'd become even more aware of this electronic underworld. I read about a group of police officers who were pointing-and-clicking their way through cyberspace to solve crimes, and I read that the management at MySpace.com had hired security teams to try to protect some of its younger members from these so-called cyber-predators. Now that I was aware of it, it seemed as if there was a new article on the subject every day. Parents were meeting with school administrators to discuss the dangers. Law enforcement officials were warning people about the types of unsavory characters who were trolling these sites—MySpace, Livejournal, Friendster, Facebook, Xanga, and so on—for potential victims.

I read that MySpace alone had more than seventy million registered users, most of them teenagers. I also heard about a special on NBC's *Dateline*, "To Catch a Predator," that used hidden cameras to trap unsuspecting cyber-predators. The men thought they had arranged meetings with underage children, only to find cameras—and law-enforcement officers—lying in wait. Among those caught? A doctor, a rabbi, and a high school teacher.

In May, *Dateline* ran another sting, this time in Florida, with similar results. Asked about the morality of soliciting sex from an underage girl, one man said, "Yes, I do see things wrong with it. But I have a lack of judgment." He seemed to be suggesting that it was beyond his control, and that that made it okay.

There was also a recent case closer to home, in Silver Spring, Maryland. A fifty-five-year-old employee of the U.S. Department of Homeland Security met a fourteen-year-old girl on the Internet and tried to lure her into a sexual relationship. The "girl" turned out to be an undercover detective, and Doyle found himself facing numerous felony charges.

There was yet another story, even more disturbing, about Justin Berry, who claimed that at age thirteen he had begun doing live sexual performances on the Internet, for older men, using a so-called webcam. The performances became increasingly explicit over time, and were said to have resulted in actual sexual encounters.

It was horrifying. It seemed as if some sort of Internet bogey-man was out there, waiting to harm our children.

Several articles pointed out that these sites were the modern equivalent of hanging out at a mall or at a soda shop. It was an easy and efficient way to meet people, kids said. You put information about yourself out there—sometimes *too much* information—and tried to make new friends through an ever-expanding network. Apparently, you were able to control the people who had access to your personal site, but that function had its limits. If someone was a friend of a friend, for example, he or she could visit your site, even though you didn't know him or her. And since everyone in the world seems to be separated from everyone else by a mere six de-grees, it wouldn't be long before *anyone* was privy to your innermost thoughts and feelings.

Suddenly I could understand the evolving paranoia. The posted revelations were often deeply personal. It was clear that many of these kids found it easier to talk about themselves online than face-to-face. They weren't as self-conscious. They didn't have to worry about their looks. They must have felt that this was some-how more meaningful, more honest, and *deeper.*

The more I thought about it, the more it struck me that this whole online phenomenon combined aspects of both voyeurism and exhibitionism. To see and be seen. I wondered how many kids were making up stories about themselves to appear more interest-ing and more alluring. I was sure there was a lot of posturing going on, and I could see the danger in that. We all hunger for attention. We all want to be noticed. As one of the articles pointed out, these kids felt as if they *had to* create profiles: *If you don't have a profile, you don't exist.*

Unfortunately, these profiles—thoughts, words, pictures— were reaching people for whom they were never intended.

On October 11, MSNBC did a piece on Taylor. One of the people they interviewed was Clint Van Zandt, a former FBI investigator. He noted that Fawley had been in a perfect position to play mind games with Taylor, whether in person or online. "At age thirty-eight, you've learned how to manipulate people. You've learned how to understand someone's concerns, anxieties, challenges (and) sense of self worth—what that might be."

They also interviewed Jim Nolan, who had been covering the case for the *Richmond Times-Dispatch*. "What's so sad and tragic about this story, and why it resonates with so many people, is because every August, every September, thousands of mothers and fathers send their sons and daughters off to school for the first time," he said. "It's an adventure. It's kind of a rite of passage. And everyone hopes when you close the door and wave good-bye and drive off campus that their child is going to be okay, that where you left them is where you're going to find them."

The network included a clip of me, talking about the day I saw Taylor for the last time, just before she made that final drive back to school. "I kissed her and hugged her," I said. "And as she walked away, I did double over in pain—physical pain. I hadn't been dealing with her being gone very well. I don't know if all of that was a premonition, or, you know, just that maternal gut feeling. But yeah, I did double over in pain."

That same day, I got a call from Ernie Myers, over at Money & King, the funeral home. The medical examiner in Richmond had just phoned to tell him that Taylor's body was on its way up. I was home, alone. The image I had in my head, and that I have still, is of a skeleton that had been mauled by wild animals and nibbled at by bugs. It is the most unimaginable of horrors, and yet I couldn't stop imagining it. I also imagined the trip my daughter was making to Vienna at that very moment, in a body bag, in the trunk of a car, and my mind kept going back to the same, harrowing questions: *How much of Taylor are they sending me? What's left of her? What is left of my beautiful baby girl?*

I called Matt to tell him that we had to make final arrangements with the funeral home, and he came by to pick me up later that day. He pulled up and I went outside and got in his car. Neither of us said anything. It was odd, but then again—what was there to say?

Ernie Myers was wonderful, a gift of a human being. He was sensitive, thorough, and thoughtful, and he walked us gently through the process. By this point, Taylor's remains had arrived, and Ernie said he would be taking them to the crematorium in Alexandria the following morning, then bringing them back to the funeral home. He didn't want us to dwell on this, so he asked us to pick a memorial card, and to decide on what we wanted it to say. There were various styles, and many sample phrases to choose from. When we were done, he told us that visitors would be signing a book as they entered, and he showed us the various books on display. I didn't like any of them, so Ernie went into a back room and returned with another one. It was the best looking of them all, and that was the one we chose.

Now we had to decide on a date for the visitation, and for the funeral service. Ernie suggested that we hold two viewings, one in the afternoon, one in the evening, and that we extend the visitation hours because there would probably be a substantial turnout. The visitation fell on October 13. "That would have been her eighteenth birthday," I told Ernie.

Ernie looked like he was about cry, but he pulled himself together and got back to business. He wanted to know if the media would be allowed inside, and I said absolutely not. I did not want them on the premises. I had nothing against them, but this was a private service, for family and friends, and I didn't want the media to turn it into something else.

I looked over at Matt and he nodded. He seemed to be in a state of shock.

The next step was picking out an urn, and we chose the most beautiful wooden urn they had. Ernie explained that Taylor's remains would be put into a sealed plastic bag, and that the bag would be placed inside the urn, which would then be screwed shut. The image was so disturbing that I felt physically ill—I thought of Taylor in there, suffocating—and I made Ernie promise to put holes in the bag. "I want her to be able to breathe," I said. I know my request might not have made any sense, but the past five weeks hadn't made any sense, either.

We rented a casket for both the visitation and the funeral. It was made of polished mahogany, and lined with white silk, and it was the most beautiful casket I'd ever seen. When Ernie asked about flowers, I told him I wanted white and red roses, but no lilies. "I hate lilies," I said. He asked if we wanted donations in lieu of flowers, and I said no. "Flowers make it beautiful," I told him.

We picked the music next. We didn't want any creepy organ music, and Matt offered to make a CD of all of Taylor's favorite songs. It was a mix of old and new: The Rolling Stones, Edith Piaf, The Corrs, Savage Garden, Marilyn Manson, The Brindley Brothers, Enya, and more. I also asked him to include "Forever Young," by Rod Stewart. Taylor and I had already decided that that was the song we would dance to at her wedding. (It had even inspired one of her screen names: ForeverYounger13.) As we sat there, planning her funeral, I tried to imagine what her wedding might have been like, and I quietly sang the lyrics in my head.

We spent about three hours with Ernie, and I made most of the decisions. With every passing minute, Matt seemed to be slipping further into shock, and by the end he just nodded and quietly agreed with everything that Ernie and I suggested. When it was time to leave, Ernie asked me to please think about any items that I would want Taylor to be cremated with, and to come back with them before the end of the day.

On the way home, Matt and I talked about the great choices we had made. It was very strange. We were creating a beautiful service for a beautiful child. It wasn't exactly the eighteenth birthday party I'd been looking forward to, but it was going to be lovely nonetheless.

When I got back inside the house, I went into Taylor's room and tried to decide what to take back to the funeral home. While I was doing this, Glynnis called and asked if she could come over with Mike and Sammy, two friends. They said something about collecting some photographs of Taylor, but I was only half listening. I was focused on finding exactly the right things for Taylor's journey.

What would she have wanted? Did she want to be dressy in heaven? Did she want to be casual? Did she want comfort clothes? Jeans? A dress? What shoes would she want to wear? Oh, that last one was easy! The high-top tennis shoes she'd just bought in New York. The other decisions took more time. I chose several photographs of Taylor, some alone, some with family and friends, and I included a poem by Lisa Hendricks, a coworker and close friend. I decided she'd want the Rolling Stones T-shirt that her uncle Michael had given her many years ago. It was threadbare, and the tongue logo had almost faded, but she loved it. I also included a pair of Capri jeans, her favorites, as well a long-sleeved, bohemian looking pullover that I'd bought for her for college.

When I was satisfied, I took everything back to the funeral home and gave it to Ernie. He said that he'd have to go through the things to make sure there wasn't anything made of metal.

"Just put in everything—please," I said. "She would have wanted all of these items with her. I need to believe that she has everything so please don't tell me if you have to leave anything out."

"Okay," Ernie said.

"And don't forget the air holes," I said.

"I won't," he said.

"Promise?"

"I promise."

When I left, I went to talk to Father Rick Lord, at the Church of the Holy Comforter, who was going to be performing the funeral service. I will never forget what he told me. "God did not take Taylor," he said. "Ben Fawley did. And God cried when Taylor died." For some reason, those words were more comforting and more meaningful to me than anything else I'd heard during the entire ordeal. I was feeling completely lost at the time, as you can imagine, and I needed to know that someone understood what was happening, because I certainly didn't. I don't have a formal religious education, and I was honestly very confused. I believed in God, then as I do now, but I was in the dark about what that meant. When Rick Lord told me that God had cried for Taylor, it somehow made sense. Taylor was my life, and God knew that. Of course He was upset.

The next day, I made my way to the mall to find an appropriate outfit for the funeral. I was numb, on autopilot—simply doing what needed to be done. I went to Lord & Taylor and found a pinstriped pant suit, and another suit that consisted of a skirt and jacket. The skirt had a pleat, and a delicate, striped pattern.

When I got home, my mom was there, arranging the flowers and balloons she had ordered for Taylor's birthday. It didn't even register. I guess my mind wouldn't let it register.

The doorbell kept ringing, and a steady stream of people came and went, bringing trays of food. I'm sure I must have eaten at some point, but I really don't remember. I do remember however, going upstairs and locking myself in my room and escaping into sleep again.

The next morning was a blur. I remember getting ready for the visitation, which was at two o'clock, and I remember Bubba Bates, the private investigator, coming for me at a little after one. He got me to the visitation in plenty of time, and Matt was already there, standing outside, looking lost and forlorn. It was a raw, overcast afternoon. I said hello to Matt and he nodded and said hello back, and then I walked inside to have a look.

I was completely gob-smacked by the flower arrangements. Every inch of space was filled with huge, beautiful bouquets of flowers, stacked behind the casket and along the walls. There were so many of them that they were even staggered up the stairs, as far as the eye could see. Ernie came out to greet me and saw the look on my face and smiled. "We received 129 flower arrangements," he said.

I ran around making a few adjustments, for my own esthetic reasons, and then I stood back to admire the beautiful room.

I now noticed that there were birthday balloons tied to the casket, and I knew right away that this had been my mother's doing. I thought this was the perfect touch. It was Taylor's eighteenth birthday, after all. She deserved balloons, not a funeral. I also noticed various posters, adorned with photographs of Taylor, and realized that this had been Glynnis's doing. I thought that was pretty perfect, too.

A few minutes before two o'clock, Matt and I went and stood in front of the casket, and a moment later people started filing inside. There was a steady stream of mourners—friends, family, and strangers—and their presence really warmed my heart. These people were there for Taylor. She had been on earth so briefly, and yet had somehow touched hundreds and hundreds of lives.

At four o'clock, Ernie shut the doors. Mom and I went back to Ann and Mike's house with family and a few friends to take a break before the next viewing. We had a little something to eat, and Mom went outside and released a few of Taylor's birthday balloons, one at a time. We watched them float away, melding into the gray sky. It was a sweet gesture, and it was Mom's way of dealing with Taylor's passing, but I had to avert my eyes—it was like watching Taylor float away from me.

After that, I asked Bubba to drive me home, and I changed and got ready for the second viewing. When we returned to the funeral home, the police were getting ready to direct traffic, and the media were camped out across the street.

It was a huge turnout. Dozens of Taylor's friends were there, and most of them were in tears. I found myself comforting them, and somehow that made perfect sense. I was preparing to lay my only child to rest, and she was right behind me, in an urn, in a casket, but as I tended to these living, breathing, weeping children, I was able to forget—if only for a few moments—the urn, the casket, and the little plastic bag with the air holes.

In total, more than a thousand people came to pay their respects, despite the rain and the long lines. We'd only been in

Vienna for four years, and I was deeply moved by this incredible show of support.

Chief Rodney Moore and two of his officers were among the mourners. When he approached, wiping his eyes, I hugged him, thanked him for coming, and introduced him to my mother. I had told my mother so many good things about Chief Monroe that she hugged him and held on for dear life. I thought she would never let him go. At one point, he whispered in her ear: "We've got our man."

When we got home that night, my mother told me what Chief Monroe had said, and I didn't even think about it. I was sure he'd been referring to Ben Fawley, and I'd known from the start that he was guilty, so this did not register as news.

The next day, Friday, October 14, we held the funeral service at the Holy Comforter Church. Father Rick Lord delivered the eulogy. He said, in part:

> I want to say to Taylor's parents, Janet and Matt, and to your entire extended family, that our hearts draw near to you today. We have come together as a community in great sorrow, for Taylor's death has put us in touch with the bonds of our common humanity. That is why so many of us have gathered in this sacred space. As the poet John Donne wrote, "Anyone's death diminishes me; because I am involved with humanity." The journey of grief puts us in touch with a universal longing of the human heart, a longing for something more, a longing to make sense of the life we live, a longing to know that death will not have the final word.

There is lurking in the back of our minds a very common and yet difficult question. If there is a God who has brought this world into being, does this God care?

Perhaps the biggest obstacle to faith is simply the way the world is. It is beautiful and it is fruitful, but it is also terrifying and dreadful things happen to innocent people. We believe that God did not create a "ready-made world," but one that is allowed to become itself, and that human beings share in this foundational creative freedom. We cherish that freedom, but with it comes a darker possibility. For there are those who selfishly choose to misuse their freedom, and the innocent suffer. "Why is this happening to me?" we ask, or "Why is this happening to someone I love?" These are entirely legitimate questions to ask. But in the end, intellectual or theological answers will only go so far. The problems of evil and suffering are not intellectual problems to be solved but existential ones that must be lived. They are problems of spiritual survival.

But I do have a particular insight to offer that has been helpful to me in my own journey and ministry with others on the road of grief. It is an insight that in some sense enables the possibility of belief in God and that God is not simply an impartial spectator looking down on this strange and suffering world. The Christian faith holds that God is a fellow sufferer, a fellow participant in the agony of creation. God has chosen to join the human journey. In Christ, God shares our human nature. He lives and dies as one of us. We witness the darkness and paradox of the Cross and we hear from the lips of the crucified a desperate cry, "My God, my God, why hast thou forsaken me?" Such a cry reveals that God knows human suffering from the inside of creation and not simply from the outside. But even more significant—in a way we cannot yet fully understand, God in Christ took our human nature through the experience we call death, and showed us that beyond death there is a risen life, an eternal kind of life that death cannot destroy.

I do believe we have a destiny beyond death. And though that doesn't explain away the suffering of this world, I think it would be far more difficult to live with hope if there were no such destiny to look forward to. If we matter to God in this life, and we do, then we must matter to God forever. If Taylor mattered to God in this life, and she did, then Taylor must matter to God forever.

Michael Fath, an old family friend, wrote an original score for the service. Friends and relatives got up and shared their memories. Glynnis Keogh said a few words. And Trevor Patch, my ex-husband, got up spoke about the "sophisticated and intelligent young lady" who at age three became his stepdaughter and changed his life. He closed by reading "Funeral Blues," the W.H. Auden poem. I can still recite the final stanza by heart:

> *The stars are not wanted now: put out every one;*
> *Pack up the moon and dismantle the sun;*
> *Pour away the ocean and sweep up the wood,*
> *For nothing now can ever come to any good.*

It was a beautiful service. About five hundred people had tried to squeeze into the church, and many of them ended up in the corridors and in a second room where they could hear everything on small speakers.

When it was over, the casket was put into a hearse and the hearse pulled away. That was the most painful moment of my entire life. My little girl was in there, leaving me—gone forever. I watched the hearse until it was out of sight, and when it disappeared from view I wondered what I had left to live for.

Bubba and George were standing at my side, and they each took one of my arms to keep me from collapsing. There was a group of reporters waiting across the way, beyond the lawn, keeping a respectful distance, and we had already decided that I should show them the courtesy of making a brief statement. We made our way across the lawn—a seemingly endless lawn—and I was sobbing before I'd even begun. Weeks earlier, some of these same reporters had been wondering when they were finally going to see me cry. Well, the wait was over. What none of them seemed to understand is that I'd been crying from the very first day, and that I'm crying still.

7

REST IN PEACE

After the service, and after the hearse pulled away, and after I broke down in front of the reporters, I returned to the church for a small reception. It was just family and close friends, and I saw people I hadn't seen in years. It did my heart good to be around so many people who had known and loved Taylor. I found myself thinking about the dozens of people I'd met over the previous weeks. Many of them had only known Taylor in passing, and some of them had never met her at all, but they had all been affected by her story, and by her brief life—they had all gone out of their way to tell me so.

Matt and I left the reception together. We rode in a hired Bentley, with a police escort, and stopped at the funeral home. Ernie Myers was waiting for us. He took us inside and gave us the urn with Taylor's ashes and we got back into the Bentley for the 20-mile drive to the cemetery. The police motorcade stayed with us for the entire trip, stopping traffic at every corner and at every light. I thought of my father, who had been a motorcade officer himself. He would have been proud of the way these men had handled themselves.

Just before we reached the cemetery, I looked down at the urn in my lap. I remembered the last time I'd been in a Bentley, almost eighteen years ago. It was the day we brought Taylor home from the hospital. We'd had champagne on that ride, to celebrate, but this time there was no champagne, and no celebration—only darkness and sorrow.

When the Bentley pulled to a stop, Matt and I got out and were directed to a little table adorned with flowers. I set the urn on the table and Matt moved off to one side to let me have a private moment with Taylor. When I was done, Matt took a private moment of his own, and then we each set a red rose on the urn and walked away. Taylor was buried next to William, her favorite cousin.

I returned to the house, where family and friends were waiting, and I had barely settled in when the phone rang. It was a reporter. He was calling to tell me that Ben Fawley had confessed, but that he had told police it was an accident. He said he and Taylor had engaged in rough sex, and that he'd inadvertently choked her.

I was so upset I could hardly catch my breath.

"Miss Pelasara?" the reporter said. "You still there?"

"Yes," I said, my voice barely a notch above a whisper.

"I hear ABC's going to run the story on the five o'clock news."

I hung up, feeling completely lost. Now I understood what Chief Monroe had meant when he told my mother that they had their man. Fawley had confessed just a day previous, which was no surprise to me—I'd known almost from the start that he was involved. The part that disturbed me was the details. I knew he was lying. Taylor would not have had consensual sex with that man. She had already made that mistake, and she would not have repeated it.

I went out to my garden, where it was quiet, and called Matt Brock, an ABC reporter I'd gotten to know in the course of the search. I asked him if the rumor was true, and he confirmed it, and I begged him—literally begged him—to wait one day before putting it on the air.

"He's lying," I said. "Fawley's lying about the sex. Please don't put that ugly image out there. I buried my daughter less than an hour ago. I'm only asking for one day. *One day.*"

Brock said that he had been asked to run the story, and that he couldn't do anything about it. I then asked him if he would be good enough to tone it down, reminding him that I'd always been there for him—every phone call, every question, every request. "I always made time for you," I said. "I've never asked you for anything, and this is a very small thing I'm asking."

"I can't," he said. "I just got word that I have to run it."

I was so upset that I cursed him and hung up. It was obvious that Brock was a reporter first, and a human being second. I was sure there were situations where that might be necessary, but I didn't think this was one of them.

I sat there, devastated, not knowing what to do, then I picked up the phone and rang Pat Collins, at NBC. He said they were working on the same story, but he listened to what I had to say, and heard me out. He would run the story, he said, because he had to run the story, but he assured me that he would tone down the sexual aspects.

At five o'clock, I watched the news with family and friends. It was gut-wrenching. We learned that on Wednesday, October 12, Fawley—against the wishes of his attorney—had spoken to police. He told them that he and Taylor had had "rough sex" in her car, and that he had accidentally restricted her breathing and caused her death. At that point, Fawley said he panicked. He had left Taylor's body in a ravine, unburied, and returned home. As we already knew, the property was adjacent to a parcel owned by the parents of an ex-girlfriend, Erin Crabill, who subsequently recognized the location from photographs on Fawley's computer.

I knew it was a lie. Taylor had had sex with Fawley, yes—but she had told several friends that it had been a mistake. Plus it didn't make any sense. Fawley lived near the campus. Why would they drive an hour and a half to a remote location to have sex in Taylor's car? Taylor had wanted nothing to do with Fawley. Again I remembered what she'd told me once, during an early visit home: "I met a guy I thought was kind of interesting, but he turned out to be a real weirdo."

All I could think was, *Ben Fawley, may you rot in hell.*

After the newscast, George called to tell me we needed to act quickly. "Some people are going to believe his lies," he said. "Taylor can't speak for herself now, so we've got to do it for her."

He put together a press conference, and I went off to face the reporters. I told them that I had learned—through conversations with a number of Taylor's friends—that the liaison with Fawley had been very brief. She had been curious about him, certainly. He was older and seemed knowledgeable and he had cultivated this whole Johnny Depp look, and perhaps Taylor had allowed herself to be seduced by it. But she later made it clear, to various friends, that the brief liaison had been a big mistake. She wasn't interested in Ben Fawley, and for the press to suggest that it was an ongoing relationship was just plain wrong. It was also hurtful to me, her mother, and disrespectful to Taylor. "Let's be clear," I said. "Ben Fawley murdered my daughter. His claim that it was accidental was just one more perversion of the truth in his ever-changing web of lies." Of the sexual relationship, I said: "She did it once out of curiosity, and then didn't want anything to do with him. He had a dark side, and Taylor wasn't a dark side kind of girl."

Some of the press reported what I told them, but others went off on bizarre tangents. Several reporters talked about "erotic asphyxiation," quoting experts on the topic. They said strangulation decreased the flow of blood to the brain, and some people found that it heightened sexual pleasure. They could share their theories if they wanted to, but I knew Taylor—and that wasn't my Taylor.

On October 28, *People* magazine hit the stands. According to the story, Fawley told the police that he had sex with Taylor at least twice. Even if that was true, I thought, that didn't constitute a relationship. The magazine also talked about Fawley's dark side, then segued into conjecture: "(H)er parents were unaware she lived a sort of secret life on the Internet." That really bugged me. Reporters kept hammering away at this Internet business, and it was getting out of hand. Matt played along, though: "It's not like hiding a diary under the mattress," he said. "Parents need to be keenly aware of what their kids are putting out there."

I wondered if I should have been more aware of Taylor's postings, but I'd read them, and—in all honesty—I didn't see any danger there. Maybe she was a little too open about herself, too revealing, and maybe I would have advised her to be more circumspect, but I don't see how that would have changed anything.

I wondered if she and Fawley had exchanged e-mails, and I wondered about the contents—what had this thirty-eight-year-old man said to my seventeen-year-old daughter to seduce her? But if there had been e-mails, and I had seen them, what could I have done? If they'd been explicit, and suggestive, I know I would have taken action. But if they were harmless exchanges between two people—what then? What action was called for?

It was all hypothetical, anyway. I knew that Taylor and Fawley must have communicated online from time to time, because one night I'd inadvertently found myself being IM'd, and IMing, Fawley, but I didn't know if any e-mails existed, and if they did they had long since disappeared into the ether.

Thinking about all the possibilities and permutations was exhausting, but the press never seemed to tire of it. Still, I resented the allegations about my daughter's "secret life." One of Taylor's entries read, "I've drifted so far from all of my old friends, and I don't think anyone noticed I was gone." Did that sound like a "secret life"? To me, it sounded like the musings of a normal, adolescent girl, simply trying to deal with the experience of being away from home for the first time.

VCU hadn't said much more about my daughter, but they, too, had joined the ongoing discussions about the Internet. VCU President Eugene Trani was quoted as saying that the administration was trying to make its students more aware of the dangers of cyberspace. "This is the most important thing we've learned from the Behl case," Trani said.

If that was the most important thing they'd learned from the case, they still had a lot to learn.

In mid-November, I drove back to Richmond to meet with the task force. We convened in a conference room at the Marriot. Those present included Doc Lyons, of the Virginia State Police, John Venuti, from the Richmond Police, and Mike Jaegles and Chris Bullard, from the District Attorney's office, who were going to help prosecute the case. I had come armed with a list of questions. I wanted to know if they had any new leads; I wanted to know what they'd learned from the forensic evidence; I wanted to know when I could expect to see the case go to trial. Unfortunately, a gag order had been imposed, so they weren't at liberty to tell me much of anything, and I found this incredibly frustrating. Every time I asked a question, Lt. Venuti had the same answer. "That's nuts-and-bolts, Janet. That's nuts-and-bolts. My hands are tied." After about the tenth time, I turned to him and said, only half joking, "I don't like you. You're a fellow Italian, and I still don't like you."

The strange thing is, I had even tried to use the room to psychological advantage, positioning myself with my back to the window so that the light would be in their eyes. I pointed this out to them, trying to show them that I had a sense of humor, and Lt. Venuti smiled. "You're going to have to make it a lot hotter than that to get us to break a gag order," he said.

I knew they couldn't share much with me, if anything, but there was one question they just had to answer, and there was no legal reason for them not to do so. I took a breath, braced myself, and asked it:

"How much of my daughter did I bury?"

The room went silent. Every man looked down at his hands, as if on cue. The silence continued, unbroken, and my heart began to sink. It wasn't fair! I deserved an answer! I needed to know!

I could feel the tears now, pouring down my cheeks and raining onto my list of questions. I slammed both hands on the table, hard, and they all looked up in unison, startled.

"I have been really patient," I said, sobbing. "I have done nothing but cooperate with you. I have repeatedly expressed my confidence in you to the media. And I'm not sitting here giving you a hard time about not answering my questions. I know what a gag order is, and I understand that you can't talk about the case. But you have to answer this one question for me. I have to know."

Doc Lyons looked across at me, clearly in pain. My tears were still raining onto the table. "Janet," he said gently. "If we could tell you, we would."

"That's not fucking good enough!" I said, exploding. "I need to know! I need to know if I buried just a head or a leg! Did I bury an arm! How much of my daughter did I bury?! How much of her could still be lost in those woods! You have to answer this for me!"

They all stared at me in silence, and once again I thought the silence would go on forever. Then Lt. Venuti spoke up. He looked me in the eye, and said, "You buried most of her, Janet. You buried most of her."

He looked shattered, as did the others. I knew that was the only answer I was going to get. It wasn't enough, but it had to be enough. There would be no more.

I went home, numb.

In the weeks ahead, I worked on Taylor's estate, on bracing myself for the coming trial, and on answering cards and letters. There was a veritable mountain of mail, and I could never get though more than three or four replies without collapsing in tears, exhaustion, or both.

I also spent a lot of time in Taylor's room, going through her things. I found two unsent thank-you notes, dating back to her graduation party. One of them was to David and Elizabeth Green, our friends in England. She hadn't had their address, so I wrote it on the envelope, in my own hand, and sent it on.

I spent Thanksgiving in Ocean City with one friend, and Christmas in Las Vegas with another, and I wasn't sure I'd survive either of them: The pain of missing Taylor was unbearable at times, and I still don't know how I made it through. I remember one day I went to a local store to buy Christmas cards, and when I realized I couldn't buy one for Taylor I began to sob. I was standing there, tears streaming down my cheeks, my nose running, but I bought one anyway. I took it out to the cemetery and left it by her grave.

As the New Year got under way, I discovered that the only thing I had to look forward to, if you can call it that, was the trial. I wanted to be there when Ben Fawley was put away for life. In a way, much as I hate to admit it, the desire for revenge really helped keep me going.

On Tuesday, January 17, Fawley was indicted for Taylor's murder. He was accused of killing Taylor while attempting to abduct and rape her, "willfully, deliberately and with premeditation."

A little over a week later, on January 25, he was taken from the Richmond City jail to the Mathews County Circuit Court, to be booked on the charges. I was there before 9:00 a.m., and I took a seat in the front row. I had hoped to see him in a prison jumpsuit, but he was wearing regular clothes. The clothes appeared too big for him, and I believe it was deliberate: When people saw him in those clothes, they would likely think he had lost a great deal of weight, and they might actually feel something akin to sympathy. I didn't feel sympathy. But I didn't feel rage or disgust or hatred, either. I didn't feel much of anything, frankly. I *wanted* to, believe me—I was tired of being numb—I wanted to feel real feelings again, even if they were the wrong kinds of feelings, but nothing came. I just felt empty, like a shell of my former self.

When I got home, I decided I wanted to write a book about my daughter. I wanted the world to know her as I had known her, and I wanted them to remember. She had been on this earth a short time, but she was an angel here and now.

While I was thinking about the book, I found myself in her room, going though her things, and I came across a single stanza from a poem that she had ripped out of an old calendar. It was from the "The Stolen Child," by William Butler Yeats:

Come away, O human child!
To the waters and the wild
With a faery, hand in hand,
For the world's more full of weeping than you can understand.

I wondered why that had spoken to her, or what it meant, and for a time I sat there, adding to the weeping of the world.

8.

GUILTY

In the days and weeks ahead, I spent a great deal of time talking to the lawyers about the coming trial, and dealing with various setbacks. The wheels of justice were moving forward, but they were grinding very slowly.

On February 13, prosecutors decided to eliminate references to rape and abduction in the indictment, partly because they still weren't sure how Taylor had died, and partly because they didn't know whether they could make a case for premeditation. The revised charges now accused Fawley of "feloniously killing and murdering Taylor Marie Behl."

I was told that the new language conformed to the definition of second-degree murder, but that the charge of first-degree murder still held—with a possible sentence of twenty years to life.

For the next couple of months, I heard nothing, then in early April I was told that Fawley had been writing letters from prison to a woman he knew, and that in one of the letters he had provided details about what had happened to Taylor on the last night of her life. A legal battle erupted over the issue of attorney-client privilege, and whether or not the letters were admissible as evidence, but I'm not sure it was ever resolved.

That same month, the trial was pushed back from May 30 to August 17. I was shattered. I wanted justice for my daughter, and I was tired of waiting. I felt as if I was in a state of suspended animation, and I didn't think I'd be able to move forward until justice had been served. I hadn't even begun to grieve yet. To be completely honest, I thought that if I allowed myself to grieve I might never recover, and I needed all my strength to make it through the trial.

In late April, I was invited to Richmond to watch Governor Timothy M. Kaine sign a number of bills that imposed tough new penalties on sex offenders.

The following June I read that someone had filed a lawsuit against MySpace.com, charging it with negligent security practices. The charges were filed by the family of a fourteen-year-old Texas girl who said she had been sexually assaulted by a nineteen-year-old man she had met online. According to the lawsuit, "MySpace.com had full knowledge that sexual predators were contacting young children on the Web site but did nothing to stop it."

Toward the end of July I went back to Richmond to meet with Jack Gill and Chris Bullard, the two prosecutors. Matt was also there. We were told that Fawley's attorney, Chris Collins, was trying to make a deal. He said Fawley might be willing to plead guilty to second-degree murder, and to serve nineteen years in prison, if the state dropped the child pornography charges. Gill and Bullard wanted more. They would only drop the pornography charges if Fawley agreed to thirty years behind bars.

I was torn. The child pornography charges weren't connected to Taylor's case, but it still didn't feel right to dismiss them. They involved a wide range of children, and it seemed as if we were willfully ignoring the crimes against them.

Neither Gill nor Bullard agreed with me. They noted that many of the children would certainly get some satisfaction from knowing that Fawley was behind bars, and they pointed out that by accepting the deal we were eliminating the possibility of an acquittal, a mistrial, or a conviction on a lesser offense, such as involuntary manslaughter.

In the end, I realized that it didn't really matter how much time Ben Fawley spent in prison. I had a feeling he was the kind of criminal who probably wouldn't survive beyond a few years, and that even if he did it was going to be a living hell. I also realized that nothing was going to bring Taylor back. I still walked into her empty bedroom every day, still hoped that none of this had really happened, and still expected the phone to ring and to hear her voice on the other end.

As it turned out, the final decision wasn't even mine to make. Fawley still had to accept the counteroffer, and the judge had to sign off on the deal, and there was no guarantee that either of these things was going to happen.

A week later, on July 26, the defense team asked for another continuance, noting that it had been ten months since Taylor's death and that they still hadn't received a final autopsy report. It seemed sort of unreal to me. *Autopsy report? What are they talking about?*

The truth is, I still hadn't fully processed the fact that Taylor was gone. I would find myself wondering why she wasn't home yet, or why I hadn't heard from her, or why she wasn't pulling into the driveway with a mountain of laundry. I wasn't in denial exactly—at least I don't *think* I was—but I was having a very hard time dealing with the implications. Taylor was never coming home again. Taylor would never see another sunset. Taylor would never fall in love, get married, or become a mother.

In my more selfish moments, I would think: *Taylor will never hug me again. I will never hear her say, "Love you more."*

I knew she was gone, of course, and every day I knew it with a little more certainty, but the passage of time didn't help. Every morning, when I got out of bed, I would walk past her room and feel a jolt of pain in my already shattered heart. I'd go downstairs and make myself a cup of coffee and fight the urge to go back upstairs and sit in her empty room. Most mornings, I failed. I would find myself standing at her door and looking at her things and remembering. I remembered the way she stretched and yawned when I woke her; the way we went through her closet together, looking for just the right outfit; the way she would look at me from across the breakfast table and review her plans for the day ahead. Now there would be no more waking up, and no more days to plan. No more hopes. No more dreams. I would still call her name when I walked through the door, but she would never answer. Never.

I felt horribly guilty, too. When I sent Taylor off to college, I had promised that these would be the best years of her life. How could I have let this happen?

And how was I going to survive without her?

I had friends and family, of course, and most of them were there for me. But it was hard to be around them. Sometimes I would see so much sadness in their eyes that I couldn't bear to look at them. Worse still, sometimes I found myself comforting *them*.

I thought, *I will never get over this.* And you know something? I was right. I won't get over this—ever. But I'll have to learn to live with it. I'll keep going. Even when I feel I can't take another step, and maybe especially when I feel I can't take another step, I'll take that other step.

At the beginning of August, the medical examiner released the autopsy report, which was inconclusive. The cause of death was listed as "Homicidal violence, type undetermined."

In her report, the pathologist noted:

Due to the condition of the remains, the cause of death cannot be determined. . . . Police provided no reports or evidence analysis that would contribute to determining the cause of death with certainty. In cases where there is no skeletal injury, an asphyxial mechanism of death is a possibility.

The disposal of the body in a remote area associated with plastic material and duct tape indicate an attempt to conceal the body.

There were also a number of details I found hard to read. She
was wearing her hooded sweatshirt and a top with sequins, her silver nose stud, and her silver ring on her left ring finger.

A few days later, the defense team's request for a continuance
was turned down—they had their autopsy report and there was no
reason for further delays. I heard from the prosecutors later that
same day. The deal was still on the table, they said, and Fawley's attorneys were taking it very seriously.

It seemed as if things were about to be resolved fairly soon, one
way or another, and I didn't honestly know how I felt about it. Part
of me was looking for this to end, but part of me was afraid, too.
After all, when it was all over, I'd be forced to get on with my life.

How was I going to manage without Taylor?

Almost obsessively, I found myself thinking about all the things
I'd no longer be doing: I wouldn't be walking into Taylor's room and
waking her. I wouldn't be cooking breakfast for her. I wouldn't take
her to the mall. I wouldn't watch her lying on her bed, doing her
homework with her cat, Spot, snuggling up against her. I wouldn't
be buying junk food for her, or giving her gas money, or doing her
laundry. I wouldn't be planning vacations with her, and I wouldn't be
telling her how happy and proud I was to have a daughter like her.

The list went on endlessly, and I didn't know how to stop myself. I would never lie with her on a sandy beach, or bake her a
birthday cake, or care for her children when she and her husband
needed a break.

One evening, I found myself sitting on her bed, reading her high school journal:

There are a great many things I hope to do in my life. I only hope that doing them makes me a better and more complete person. I have tons of memories about my life; things I've done, people I've met, and places I have visited. I wish there was some way I could share this with everyone I meet. When I tell my life story it sounds like complete bullshit. Half the stuff I say, I have to admit, is bullshit. No one seems to notice, or care if they do.

I need to learn to get out of my bullshitting habits and learn to be real with people. Not to act so god-damn superior, like I have some golden stick up my ass. I have doubts about who I am. Who am I?

I know my name is Taylor Marie Behl, I know I was born October 13, 1987. I know that my mother is Janet Lynn Pelasara and my father is Matthew James Behl. I'm aware I need to learn to face the consequences of my actions. I know I can be a lazy son of a bitch. I know I feel like I'm searching for where I belong. Maybe none of us actually feel like we belong. I don't know. I don't even think I belong in my own family sometimes. . . .

I think I'm out in the world looking for my equal. Someone who is strong, independent, maybe a little lazy and bossy. Or maybe I act that way because I've always been told that's the way I am. But deep down I don't think I'm a hopeless doormat that wants to be told what to do. But who's to say I'm not?

I need to learn to connect with people. I need to learn how to make and keep a friendship. I know I'm in high school and I'm probably never going to see most of these people again, but it would be good practice. How do you learn to connect to people? Trial and error? Out of a self-help book? By observation? I have no idea! Or is it that people are just supposed to be drawn together, their personalities act like magnets and just magically draw them together.

Or should we just be ourselves out there, vulnerable and alone? That way there is no bullshit, only real human contact. I could use some human contact soon!

Is it impossible to find your perfect partner? Tall, dark, and handsome? Right? I don't know if this is what every girl dreams of, I know it's not what I look for. I find myself attracted to cocky, insecure men. Yes, men. . . . Whoever said "Girls look for men like their Daddies" wasn't far from the truth. . . .

Everyone likes to be beautiful every so often. I do! I love to put on an outfit and go out. Then I feel beautiful. Some days I just feel beautiful hanging out in my P.J.'s. Not everyday is a beautiful day. Some days I should just stay inside with the curtains closed. But people should take the good with the bad.

Eventually, I got around to doing the one thing I'd been avoiding for weeks: choosing a headstone. I went to Kline Memorials, in nearby Manassas, determined to find something simple and elegant—something that reflected Taylor's personality. Matt had already picked out the stone, pink granite, and I asked a local artist to etch a crescent moon and a fairy into the stone. I also chose the inscription:

TAYLOR MARIE BEHL
Our Bright, Beautiful and Precious Child
Oct. 13, 1987 ♥ Sept. 5, 2005
Love You More
Mom and Dad

When the headstone was done, I went out to the cemetery to see it, alone, and I braced myself, expecting to fall apart. But I didn't fall apart. I thought it looked very beautiful, and I knew that Taylor would have approved. I'm sure she was watching me at that moment, and I know she was smiling.

In the days and weeks ahead, while I waited to see whether Ben Fawley was going to take the deal, I was constantly in and out of doctors offices. One doctor for the migraines, another for my high blood-pressure, a third to adjust my anti-depressants, a fourth to talk about my feelings. This last one was wasting her time. There was nothing to talk about. There were no feelings. Without Taylor, I was empty.

Early in August, I heard from Chris Bullard, who said Fawley was probably going to take the deal. He told me we would find out on Wednesday, August 9, at the Mathews County Courthouse, in the town of Mathews.

The morning I left for Mathews, the *Richmond Times-Dispatch* reported on its website that Fawley was going to appear in court that afternoon. They said he was expected to plead guilty to second-degree murder.

I drove my own car down from Vienna. I met my sister Debbie there, along with two sets of cousins—Ann and Mike Davis and

Wayne and Karen Martin. Taylor's friend Glynnis Keogh was also there, with her sister, Aletha, and their mother, Eileen Warner. Other friends included Kay Rosenthal, Karen Fones, Jan Godfrey, Elizabeth Stockton, Carolyn White, and Julie and Steve Crabill.

When we went into the courtroom, I sat between Debbie and Glynnis. I turned as Fawley was brought inside. He was wearing a white dress shirt and dark pants. He wasn't handcuffed, but his ankles were shackled. I was filled with hatred. I had never felt such hatred in my life.

After some back and forth between the judge and the opposing teams of lawyers, Jack Gill took center stage. He read the summary of evidence against Ben Fawley, and it took him an hour and half to get through it. I'd been warned beforehand that I wasn't going to like much of what I heard, and I'd been told to try to disregard key elements of the confession, particularly the section detailing Taylor's death. Most of it had been concocted by Fawley, and much of it was contradictory.

I don't know how I sat through it. Even Jack Gill had to pause from time to time to compose himself.

The following is a portion of what was read in court:

18) On September 15, 2005, Ben Fawley was interviewed by the FBI. He stated that Taylor came to his house, he believed, at about 4:15 p.m., a time when Taylor was actually in the process of leaving Northern Virginia. Fawley claimed that he and Taylor had sex at his apartment and that he walked her up to meet another guy. According to the defendant, Taylor came by to borrow a skateboard and

they had sex again. Fawley stated that he walked Taylor back to her dorm where she got rid of her purse. They walked back to Fawley's apartment and he gave her a skateboard and she left. Fawley again gave his story of being abducted the morning of Taylor Behl's disappearance. Mr. Fawley stated that he and Taylor had participated in light bondage and that his bed is set up for light bondage. Fawley denied having anything to do with Taylor's disappearance and stated that he wanted her found.

19) On September 16, 2005, during the execution of a search warrant at his apartment, Ben Fawley stated, "I have nothing to hide about Taylor. I'm worried about Taylor. I'm scared to death about Taylor." And, "Taylor's been missing for how long? Hopefully she's okay. I'm hoping she's okay. I'm scared because it's so much attention and she hasn't turned up. But if I had done something to Taylor, first thing I would do is run like hell."

20) On September 17, 2005, Taylor Behl's vehicle was discovered on Mulberry Street in Richmond, Virginia.

21) On September 21, 2005, two witnesses observed Ben Fawley in his apartment with gloves "frantically polishing" two firearms. He stated that he was doing it because if Taylor was found dead, he did not want there to be any connection between the guns and her (Tracy Herman transcript, p. 47). The guns shortly thereafter came into the custody of the Richmond Police Department.

22) On September 23, 2005, after having been advised of his rights, Ben Fawley made statements to Investigator Les

Lauziere. He stated that he "did a fetish movie in June in Charlottesville." Fawley stated that Taylor had left his apartment the evening she disappeared. He knew this because the skateboard he left her was gone from the top of the stairs at his apartment. He claimed that he had worked on his computers that night and left his apartment around the time it was getting light to walk up the street to the Lee Monument. He said that Taylor said that she was going to meet Kevin at the Village Café and had to be there before closing time to get served. He stated that "Taylor never lied to me." He stated, "You can't put me in jail for Taylor because I didn't do anything to her." He told Investigator Lauziere that he was trying to be honest with him. He stated, "I'm hoping she got fed up and ran off," and "I don't even want to think about that," "she's a nice kid." He stated, "Taylor is missing, her car is gone, they're not connected. One thing I can tell you is that Taylor was missing before her car was." He then claimed that he and Taylor were going to make her car disappear and that he had stolen a license plate to put on it. Fawley stated that he dropped her off to see her boyfriend, went and stole the plate and that he had the license plate and skateboard for her when she came to his apartment. He stated it was still daylight outside when he left her with her boyfriend. Fawley stated that before he dropped her off to see her boyfriend, that Taylor had come by and that they had gone to the Fulton Gas Works in Shockoe Bottom to break in. He said they "chickened out." He stated that while they were out, he and Taylor had sex in the car three times near the Fulton Gas Works—"in the front seat, in the back seat, and in the trunk." He stated it was light outside. Fawley stated that he and Taylor "had relations" several times that day, including at his apartment. Fawley claimed that Taylor showed up at his place sometime after 9 p.m. and that he walked her back to her dorm and waited for her out front. He stated that he left her a bag with a wrench and screwdriver in it along with the skateboard. He stated that later that same day her car was gone. He only learned of her being missing from the VCU police. He said that he "Started to worry when I didn't hear from her," and that she was supposed to call him from a friend's cell phone. He stated that Taylor had a plan to take her car out of state and make it disappear. Fawley said that "Taylor never upset me." He said "that night (he) was not fit to leave (his) apartment," and "the point when (he) left Taylor . . . drugs started kicking in after I left her dorm." He claimed he last saw her in a black tank top and that she was not wearing a hoodie. He said Kevin was the last person to see Taylor and that he later went looking for Kevin. Fawley claimed that after he got back from Taylor's dorm, he was sitting at his computer desk.

23) On October 5, 2005, Sgt. Gary Natoli and Detective Chris Beville of the VCTJ police, were tracking down information gleaned from Ben Fawley's computers. A

photograph from a dirt road off of Knightwood Road in Mathews County, Virginia, labeled "Home Sweet Home" was shown to Ben Fawley's former girlfriend who identified the photograph as being a heavily wooded property next to her parents' home. Sgt. Natoli and Detective Beville, accompanied by the female, walked down the dirt road located on this property roughly ½ mile where the road ended in one direction and turned off to the left. Just after the turn, Sgt. Natoli and Detective Beville discovered the body of Taylor Marie Behl, buried in a shallow ditch in a plastic tarp, still clothed in a bra, shirt, and hoodie. No pants or underwear were found on the body or at the site.

24) The evening of October 12, 2005, Ben Fawley summoned law enforcement to the Richmond City Jail and made a statement to Richmond Police Detectives Jason Hudson and James Simmons with his attorney present. He was read his Miranda rights and signed a waiver form. His statement on this occasion was inconsistent with all of his prior statements. In contrast to his September 23, 2005, statement, Fawley did not claim that he and Taylor Behl went to the Fulton Gas Works and had sex three times in her car before he walked her to Bowe Street. Rather he stated that she came to his apartment unannounced and after complaining about being dumped by her boyfriend she asked to be tied up again, something not mentioned in any of his prior accounts. Also new to this version, Fawley claimed that she asked him to put his hand over her

mouth. Fawley said that while they were having sex, her phone rang and he had to untie her. He stated that he and Taylor "finished up," and he walked her to Bowe Street at her request. Fawley stated that Taylor was asking him to either make her car disappear or to assist him in a break in. Fawley stated that he parted company with Taylor shortly after arriving at Bowe Street and leaving her with the other guy. Fawley stated that he called her afterwards and told her to meet him at 9 p.m., that he was willing to do what they had discussed. While Fawley's prior statements ended with Taylor Behl picking up a skateboard and leaving, in this account the defendant said that Taylor came over and that they "fooled around" on his bed and then he walked her back to her dorm. Along the way, Fawley said that they agreed to break into an abandoned building. According to Fawley, Behl briefly went into her dorm, returned, and they walked back to his apartment. They left in her car in search of a building to break into. Fawley described the search for a place to break into. He claimed that after one stop that he and Taylor started "fooling around" and that she wanted him to put a bag over her mouth. He claimed that when it did not work that Taylor started berating him. Fawley proposed that they go to the beach at which he had previously visited with a former girlfriend. The beach is located in Mathews County. Fawley claimed that they got lost along the way, parked, and had sex again. He claimed that Taylor asked him to tie her up again and he did and that she told him to put the bag over her mouth and let her pass out. Fawley stated that upon arrival at the beach that he opened the door because it was hot. He stated that he and Taylor climbed into the back seat and that the back rear passenger door was open. He claimed that she took her pants and underwear off, that they began having sex and that she again asked him to put the bag over her mouth. Fawley claimed that Taylor had talked to people online about it. He stated that Taylor started choking and that he took the bag off. Fawley claimed that she began berating him again, stating that he didn't have the guts to let her pass out. Fawley stated that "things got crazy." He stated that Taylor told him that if he didn't let her help him break into a business that she was going to call her mom and tell her mom that he had raped her. Fawley stated, "I flipped out. And I remember at one point I was sitting up on the back seat of the car and I was crying and she was stuck between the seats and had me pinned against the seat. She was bent with her head toward the front . . . and she was all tied up because we tied her up for sex." Fawley claimed that he was trying to pull her up in order to find what she was choking on and that he got her up on the seat and "she wasn't choking any more and I realized she had peed herself." Fawley claimed Taylor was not responding and stated that he jumped in the front seat and raced back towards Richmond. Later in the interview Fawley said that Taylor had first been tied with her hands above her head onto the door handle and that later her hands were tied with duct tape behind her back. He stated that she kept her bra and shirt on; Fawley said that when he got back to Richmond, he covered her over with a blanket in the back seat while he went up to his apartment looking for anything that she had left in the apartment. He stated that he drove out near the airport and parked on a dead end road, took the cell phone battery out of Taylor's phone and dropped both the phone and battery outside of the car. Taylor's cell phone was subsequently recovered by law enforcement. Fawley said he sat in the car and put "the small .38" in his mouth. Though he did not mention in his initial narrative that he got the gun when he went back to the apartment after arriving back in Richmond, when asked the question, Fawley asserted that this was the case and that he had not had it when he first left with Taylor. Fawley stated that he put two trash bags over Taylor and put her in the trunk and drove back out to a dirt road. This was the dirt road off of Knighthood Road. Fawley said he again put the gun in his mouth, and then realized he wasn't going to kill himself. He said he took Taylor out of the trunk, sat her down and covered her with some branches and leaves and drove home. Fawley admitted that his report of being abducted was false. He said that he cleaned Taylor's car with bleach, vacuumed it, and washed it down inside and out. Fawley stated that he was a violent drunk and had a "mean temper." Fawley stated that he subsequently went back to the woods and dug a hole that was not very deep and buried Taylor. Asked to recount the part of the story at the beach, this time Fawley stated that he performed oral sex on Taylor. He stated that she asked to have her legs tied up because she was tired of holding them. He stated that because the strips of fabric weren't long enough, they decided to duct tape her legs, each leg separately, in a bent position. He stated that she continued to ask him to put his hands over her mouth. Despite having said that Taylor was tired of holding her legs, Fawley then stated that Taylor's hands were tied above her head at this point. Fawley claimed that Taylor then said she wanted to feel like she was being kidnapped so she wanted him to "really tie her up." Fawley said he tied her hands behind her back. He said he had the bag over her mouth, but then took it off, which made Taylor angry. Fawley said that she wanted to be put in the trunk so he put the back seat down and put her in the trunk. Fawley said he climbed into the trunk through the front of the car and that they began to have sex again. Fawley said that this was not working and that she began asking him again about robbing a business. He said that they got back into the back seat and that Taylor wanted to try the bag over her mouth again. Fawley said he put the bag over her mouth and then took it off again and that Taylor then started "cussing" him out, calling him a wimp. He stated that Taylor then said "choke me," and that she wanted to gasp for air and to think she was going to die. Fawley said that Taylor continued to berate him about various issues and that she then said she was going to tell her mom and the police that he raped her. Fawley stated that the next thing he remembered was being stuck half off of the seat and Taylor in a sideways position choking. He stated that he could not remember whether she still had the bag on. Fawley stated that the second time he tried to bury Taylor that he thought that he took the tape off of her hands. When asked what happened in between the time he flipped out and the time he heard Taylor choking, Fawley stated, "I think I might of put my hands over her mouth and told her to shut up." Fawley said that he remembered telling her to shut up, that it wasn't rape, and that it wasn't "something to joke about." He stated that he remembered her saying, "You're gonna let me help you rob the store or I'm gonna tell. You're gonna let me help you or I'm gonna tell, I'm gonna tell." The defendant then stated that he "flipped out like this with Kit and Kit says I tried to strangle her." When asked what happened when he flipped out with Taylor, Fawley stated, "But that's the problem, I don't know what happened when I flipped out on Kit, only Kit knows. And I don't know what happened when I flipped out at that point with Taylor. All I re-member, like I said, was the next thing I recall was trying to get her onto the seat. I don't remember anything." He stated that "why I'm here right now is because of what goes on in my head. What always goes on in my head and it won't stop. . . . It's why after I had the fight with the Polish girl . . . I had myself committed because I don't remember what happened when I had the fight with the Polish girl." THE COMMONWEALTH INTRODUCES FAWLEY'S RIGHTS WAIVER FORM, RECORDED STATEMENT AND A TRANSCRIPT COLLECTIVELY AS COMMONWEALTH'S #9.

25) Deputy Sheriff Tucker at the Richmond City Jail reported that after the defendant returned from making his statement, he stated that "the situation is a game of chess; I made my move, now it's time for the police to make their move."

26) The Commonwealth would have produced evidence of prior bad acts for the purpose of showing intent and lack of mistake. Mr. Fawley's statements comparing his state of mind—flipping out and not remembering—in the prior acts to his state of mind in this case, in which he claimed again not to remember, provided the logical connection or nexus to the prior acts. The Commonwealth would have produced evidence that in the previous cases, just as in this case, Mr. Fawley became upset with the victims, physically assaulted them by cutting off their air supply and that afterwards he threatened suicide. The Commonwealth would have shown that there was no claim at the time of having blacked out or not remembered the event and that in one instance he told the victim he "didn't mean to" and admitted to the police that he had in fact put his hands on the victim.

27) The Commonwealth would have introduced evidence to show that despite Fawley's assertion as to how hot it was in the vehicle that evening and his statement that Taylor had on her shirt and bra, she not only had her bra and shirt on, but her hoodie as well. In addition, duct tape was found on the outside wrist of the left sleeve of the hoodie.

28) The Commonwealth would have produced evidence by Lt. Buck Garner of the Louisa County Sheriff's department, which provided items belonging to Taylor Behl. Lt. Gamer has been qualified as an expert before in Virginia's courts and the Commonwealth would have had him recognized as such in this case. Lt. Garner's bloodhound Chess was exposed to the articles belonging to Taylor Behl. The dog, who is trained only to detect the scent left by living individuals (air scent across $1/4$ acre of woods) then picked up a strong scent of Taylor Behl halfway down the dirt road where her body was found and all the way to the grave site area. Lt. Gamer would have testified that in his opinion, his dog's strong reaction indicated that Taylor Behl was alive on the dirt road, and that her scent was a strong fear scent. COMMONWEALTH'S EXHIBIT #10.

29) The Commonwealth would have established by means of DNA testing and dental records that the body recovered from the ditch off of the dirt road leading from Knightwood Road that Mr. Fawley referenced as that of Taylor Behl, was in fact Ms. Behl.

30) The Commonwealth would have shown through trace evidence and DNA that hairs taken from the body bag, tarp, plastic and duct tape surrounding Taylor Behl's body were those of Ben Fawley. This evidence would have also shown that Taylor Behl's hair was found on these items.

31) Forensic evidence would have shown the presence of blood on Taylor Behl's bra, shirt and jacket. Due to the breakdown of cells in the blood, DNA was not found in these samples.

32) THE COMMONWEALTH MOVES TO INTRODUCE THE FBI LAB EXAMINATIONS THAT ESTABLISH THESE FACTS COLLECTIVELY AS COMMONWEALTH'S #11.

33) The Commonwealth's evidence would have shown that Dr. Deborah Kay from the Medical Examiner's Office performed an autopsy on Taylor Behl's body and that her conclusion was that the Manner of Death of Taylor Behl was homicide, and the cause of death was Homicidal Violence, type undetermined. ADMIT THE AUTOPSY AS THE COMMONWEALTH'S #12.

34) The Commonwealth would have produced evidence from the nurse practitioner who performed Taylor's last physical examination and found her to be in good physical health without any reason to believe that she would suffer a sudden or unexpected death. The Commonwealth would have then produced evidence that stood in stark contrast to the statements made by Ben Fawley and his portrayal of Taylor Behl.

35) In addition to previous testimony which established a timeline of Taylor's day that would have made sex with Fawley during the periods that he claimed impossible at times because her whereabouts were otherwise established, and improbable during others because of the records of her activity, forensic examinations of Taylor Behl's computer and online activity by Richmond Police and the Attorney General's Office would have shown that these records were utterly bereft of any evidence to show that Taylor Behl had any interest in bondage or erotic asphyxiation. Jacob Cunningham and a prior boyfriend would have testified that there was nothing of the sort in their relationships with Taylor. One of Taylor's closest confidants would have testified that neither of these subjects were ever mentioned to him.

36) The Commonwealth would have shown however, that Ben Fawley had a bondage bed that he constructed in his apartment and that his name was listed as a registrant at a fetish convention in Tampa, Florida.

37) A Forensic Nurse Examiner who performed an examination of Fawley after his arrest reported that during the examination Fawley said that he was into bondage.

38) FAWLEY LETTERS—READ paragraph from Nov. 7 letter. ENTER AS COMMONWEALTH'S #13.

39) In addition, the Commonwealth's evidence would have shown that Taylor had no interest in Mr. Fawley at the time of her death outside of friendship:

a. Nick Brown, a confidant of Taylor's, would have testified that as early as May of 2005, she expressed to him that her encounter with Fawley earlier in the year had been a mistake and that she regretted it. She further said that it was "pointless" to have sex without love.

b. During her second day at VCU, Taylor and her roommate walked together to Taylor's car, which she parked near Ben Fawley's residence because she did not have a parking spot on campus. Her roommate would have testified that Taylor expressed to her that she felt obligated to say hello to Fawley because he was watching her car, even though she did not want to because he was "weird."

c. Taylor's roommate and Jacob Cunningham would have testified that Taylor and Jacob spent nearly every waking hour together during the time that Taylor was in Richmond.

d. After a breakup of less than a day, Taylor desired to, and did, reconcile with Jacob at dinner prior to her disappearance. A college friend would have testified that he commented on how happy she looked as she and Jacob came back to her dorm. The evidence would have shown that Taylor was smitten with Jacob as given by the testimony of Janet Pelasara and by Taylor's journal entries. . . .

e. Finally, in contrast to what Ben Fawley's assertions were concerning Taylor's attitude towards her parents,

her final diary entry begins, "I am loved uncondition-
ally by my mom and dad," and ends with the passage, "I
love my parents with my whole heart."

I love my parents with my whole heart.

Thank you, Taylor. I love you with my whole heart, too, even
though it's broken beyond repair.

When Jack Gill was finished, Fawley's lawyers entered a so-
called *Alford Plea*. Fawley was not admitting guilt, but he was ac-
knowledging that prosecutors had enough evidence to convict him.

The judge exchanged a few words with Fawley, asking if he was
in agreement with his attorneys, and Fawley nodded and said he
was, but he didn't have the courage to look the judge in the eye.

He was sentenced to forty years in prison, with ten of them
suspended. He would only become eligible for parole after he
turned sixty-five.

As they led him away, his shackles clanking, I cried out, "Mur-
derer!" I know he heard me, but he didn't acknowledge it.

I left the court with Debbie and Glynnis and lit a cigarette and
tried to process what had just happened. I think I had expected
something to change, something monumental, but nothing had
changed. Taylor was *still* never coming home.

There were a number of reporters there, and I spoke to them,
and the tenor of their questions made me realize that they, too, had
expected monumental changes. People often talk about "closure,"
and I'm not sure I ever understood what it meant. I still don't understand it. I felt no relief whatsoever. I was angry and bitter. At
one point, I remember saying that I hoped Fawley's new friends in

prison "loved him to death," and I meant it at the time, but that didn't change anything either.

When the press left, Jack Gill and Chris Bullard asked me to accompany them back to their office. It looked just like those rooms look on TV—with computers and evidence charts on the walls and maps of the city and mountains of paper everywhere. They took me aside and very solemnly gave me a small box made of white silk, with a tiny gold tassel on top. I opened the box. The silver band I'd given Taylor was inside, along with her nose stud. I thanked them and slipped the box into my purse and didn't cry.

That night, my friends and family took me to dinner at a small, local restaurant. I missed Taylor. I tried to get used to the idea that I would miss her for the rest of my life. I remember thinking, *I will survive, but I will never recover.*

Weeks later, I found myself sitting at home, in front of my computer, studying the jumble of notes that eventually became this book. I found myself struggling to find a happy ending, because people like happy endings, but there was no happy ending in sight.

I asked myself, as I have ten thousand times in the past year, whether I would have done anything differently—whether I *could* have done anything differently—and the answer remained the same: *No.* I wasn't the perfect mother, certainly, but I was the best mother I could be, and I'd like to think that that was good enough.

I didn't have enough time with Taylor, but I am immensely grateful for the time I did have. I am proud of everything she was, and proud of everything she was becoming.

In her high school journal, Taylor wrote that she wanted to be a "worldly woman, strong and independent. I want to be the one people go to when they need help. I want to be tough and kind, strong but still gentle and tender. I don't want my life dictated to me, I don't want to have too many limitations. I want to be able to walk, stand, and run on my own two feet. . . . I want to be able to make it on my own."

Oh Taylor. My sweet Taylor. You would have been everything you wished for, and then some. I'm so sorry you never got that chance.

ACKNOWLEDGMENTS

From the bottom of my broken heart, I would like to give my deepest and most sincere thanks to the following people:

Ann and Mike Davis—I couldn't have made it without you; my mom, who understood; Chief Monroe and the entire team of investigators, for believing me and never giving up; George Peterson, my advisor on so many issues—for all you did and all you continue to do; Jeffrey Pelasara, you make a sister proud; my incredible and enduring family, for their constant, tireless support; Bo, for letting me lay Taylor to rest next to your son, William; Cindi and Jamey, whose open door and cozy bed got me through many difficult days and nights; Kay Rosenthal, for always being there—I love you; Bubba Bates, PI, bodyguard and dear friend; Roscoe and Diane McGhee, for turning your home into a haven; the wonderful staff at the Richmond

Marriot, whose generosity, love, and hugs helped me through those three harrowing weeks; Erin Crabill, for your courage and endurance—promise me that you'll be good to yourself; Steve Crabill, friend and self-appointed caretaker—thank you for tending to the Mathews County site; Glynnis, for being such a good and decent friend to my baby—I love you; Scarborough and Johnson, CPAs extraordinaire; the community of Pawley's Island, for its generous support; my babysitters: Dawn Wolfrey (the best appreciation dancer), Tracy Nelson (the funniest person I know), and Angie Armenakis (friend of many years, who has been with me through countless ups and downs); Skippy, whose love for me and Taylor brought us so much happiness; Sissy Hayden, for your many delicious meals-on-wheels; Jammin' Java and the Town of Vienna, for your unflagging and generous support; all the unknown people who reached out to me on the Internet and in their cards and letters and through their gifts—you have no idea how much it meant to me, and how much it means to me still; Jonathan, for that generous, much-needed gift; Susan, for the Ts we proudly wear in honor of Taylor; Joanna Massey and Joetox—bless you both; Pat Collins, Matt Brock (I have *almost* forgiven you), and Gary Reels—thank you for your interest in Taylor's story; Greta Van Susteren, for your kindness, and for introducing me to Joel, who introduced me to Judith Regan, who introduced me to Pablo Fenjves, my collaborator (and unlicensed therapist). Thanks also to Kelli and Donna, of the Victim's Assistance Program, and to Jack Gill and "Esquire" Bullard, patient, big-hearted gentlemen with kind souls—and pretty damn good lawyers to boot.

Finally, to my daughter, Taylor: You always made me feel like the luckiest and proudest mom in the world. You're in my heart forever, and you'll remain Forever Young.